When, in 1971 our then Deputy Chairman, Sir James Mackay, introduced the first edition 3
of *Highland Birds* he said:

'With *Highland Birds* we are setting out on an ambitious project in our publications field.
Our aim is simple: to establish a useful and authoritative Highland library. This library
will tell, in words and pictures, what the Highlands and Islands are and contain, without the
romance and emotion so often associated with them, but with a great deal of scholarship and
authority. We feel that this will make a significant contribution to the future status of the
region. Accurate knowledge leads to understanding and interest, and interest can lead to all
sorts of developments.

'For this first book we commissioned Desmond Nethersole-Thompson, well known in the
world of ornithology for his many years of thorough and painstaking research in the
Highlands. He has devoted a great deal of time to this enterprise—far beyond the strict
duties of an author. This the Board appreciate and, for it, we record our gratitude.

'Our thanks are due, too, to the host of individuals and organisations who have helped us,
even in the smallest way, to realise our aim in such an exciting publication. Like so much of
the story of Highland development, this is truly a co-operative enterprise. We only wish
that we could mention by name all those who helped. We and they, however, know just how
much work was involved. As you read and use this book I am sure that, like us, you will
grow to appreciate that effort.'

There is little I need add. The success of the first edition is a matter of record. Desmond
Nethersole-Thompson has brought this second edition up to date. We are convinced that
many more members of the public at home and abroad will wish this book to be readily
available for the years to come.

A. Forsyth   Member of the Board

Inverness 1974

Acknowledgements

Maimie and I have written this second edition together and we warmly thank many friends who helped us, particularly: Donald Bremner, A. Currie, J. Currie, George Dunnet, M. J. P. Gregory, C. G. Headlam, I. and M. Hills, David Lea, Donnie Macdonald, Ian Newton, John Parslow, Derick Scott, Bobby Tulloch, George Waterston and Adam Watson.

I do not forget those who did so much for the original book:

Hugh Blair, J. Morton Boyd, R. V. Collier, J. Cuss, R. D. King, J. McFadden, Mrs J. Morrison, M. F. M. Meiklejohn, N. Picozzi, D. A. Ratcliffe, D. M. Stark and the late John Markham.

D.N-T.

The Highlands and Islands Development Board gratefully acknowledges use of photographs as follows:

J. Arnott: page 106. H. Auger: front cover, pages 15, 92 (l). R. Balharry: pages 20 (l), 23 (c), back cover. H. Burton: page 20 (r). J. T. Fisher: pages 31, 45 (r), 47 (r), 70, 72, 93, 95 (r). A. Gilpin: page 85. S. Gordon: page 53. W. Higham: page 37. H. R. Lowes: pages 71 (r), 79. J. A. McCook: page 21 (l). L. MacNally: page 9. J. Markham: pages 22 (r), 34, 42 (r), 47 (l), 48 (l), 77, 94 (r). Maylott Studios Ltd: page 94 (t). D. Merrie: page 48 (r). C. K. Mylne: pages 20 (c), 23 (r), 65, 66 (l), 66 (r), 69 (l). J. Nicholson: pages 68 (l), 96 (r). C. E. Palmar: pages 24, 55, 57, 67 (c), 68 (r), 101. D. C. Palmar: page 91 (r). I. D. Pennie: page 96 (c). N. Picozzi: pages 18, 21 (r), 43, 95 (l). S. C. Porter: page 100. D. A. Ratcliffe: pages 23 (l), 41, 42 (l), 45 (c), 94 (l), 96 (l). J. Rowbottom: pages 45 (l), 67 (r), 91 (l). A. Tewnion: pages 19 (l), 83, 91 (c). B. Tulloch: pages 8, 19 (r), 44 (r), 67 (l), 69 (c), 69 (r), 71 (l), 71 (c), 87, 89, 90, 92 (r), 105. T. Weir: pages 6, 22 (l). G. Young: pages 17, 44 (l), 46. Abbreviations: (l)=left; (c)=centre; (r)=right; (t)=top.

List of some First Schedule birds

If you wish to photograph or disturb at the nest any birds listed in the First Schedule of the Protection of Birds Acts (1954-1967) you will require a permit which can be obtained from The Nature Conservancy, 19 Belgrave Square, London, S.W.1. Here are some of the birds nesting in the Highlands which receive this special protection: divers (all species), slavonian grebe, scaup, goldeneye, common scoter, greylag goose, whooper swan, golden eagle, goshawk, hen harrier, osprey, peregrine, merlin, spotted crake, dotterel, whimbrel, black-tailed godwit, wood sandpiper, greenshank, Temminck's stint, red-necked phalarope, snowy owl, wryneck, chough, crested tit, fieldfare, redwing, bluethroat, crossbill and snow bunting.

4

A Personal Note

Desmond Nethersole-Thompson (signature)

Highland Birds has been enthusiastically received. We have had letters from all over Britain and from the Soviet Union, Finland, Europe, Egypt, Africa and U.S.A. Best of all, young ornithologists have liked it. I warmly thank Sir Andrew Gilchrist and his Board for their support.

Since *Highland Birds* was published in 1971 there have been great changes. Then North Sea Oil was a cloud no bigger than a man's hand. Now the oil boom has already produced many project proposals. They plan to build complexes on many parts of our wonderful coast and close to some of the finest sea-bird and wildfowl haunts in Western Europe. Although the giant yards at Nigg and Ardersier are already there, we have not yet declared any National Nature Reserves in the Moray Firth. Orkney, Shetland, Wester Ross, Caithness and Sutherland are now also in the front line. We really must have a balanced overall plan with some places left inviolate.

These vast industrial developments have synchronised with a most dynamic phase in bird history. The southerly movement of boreal birds continues. Since the first edition, Temminck's stints have nested in Easter Ross, whimbrels in North Sutherland, and the great snowy owls are prospecting new nesting haunts in the Highlands and Islands. Waxwings have summered and shore larks have already possibly nested. Fieldfares are now well established on the mainland and the ospreys are back in Sutherland, where Victorians shot and robbed them out. The Nature Conservancy has declared the Gualin Nature Reserve in north-west Sutherland and the R.S.P.B. has reserves in the Insh Marshes in Spey Valley and on the fine sea-bird island of Copinsay in Orkney. They also have three grand moorland reserves there. The Scottish Wildlife Trust now also manages a good reserve near Golspie. But this is only a beginning.

In March 1971 I fulfilled a dream. After visiting Orkney and spending a morning on Fair Isle, we flew to Shetland, bumping down on Foula in a snowstorm, and spying on the snowy owls of Fetlar from the air! I spent an unforgettable weekend with Bobby Tulloch and the marvellous sea-bird colonies of Yell and Fetlar. Unst was much as I had always expected; but it has already changed much since Saxby and the old naturalists. I watched ravens taking the rook's niche in some of the fields near Baltasound. The sea-bird groups of all these magic northern isles, and those on the mainland sea cliffs, will soon be under threat from oil slicks.

Although I have not yet worked on all the western Isles, my sons Bruin and Patrick have camped on Colonsay, Jura, Rum and North Uist, with the Schools Hebridean Society Expeditions. They have given me valuable notes.

Jim Grassie, Gordon Lyall and Bill Mackay have been our enthusiastic friends in this enterprise. They have always been determined to make *Highland Birds* a success.

Selected Bibliography

6

AINSLIE, J A & ATKINSON, R (1937) Breeding Habits of Leach's Fork-tailed Petrel, *Brit. B.*, 30: 234-48.
ATKINSON-WILLES, G L (1963) *Wildfowl in Great Britain*, London.
BALFOUR, E (1960) The Hen Harrier in Orkney, *Bird Notes*, 30:69-73. (1968) Breeding Birds of Orkney, *Scot. B.*, 5:89-104.
BANNERMAN, D (1953-63) *The Birds of the British Isles*, 12 Vols., Edinburgh and London.
BAXTER, E V and RINTOUL, L J (1953) *Birds of Scotland*, 2 Vols., Edinburgh and London.
BOOTH, E T (1877-79) MS diaries.
BOURNE, W R P (1957) Birds of the Island of Rhum, *Scot. Nat.*, 69:21-31.
BOYD, J M (1958) Birds of Tiree and Coll, *Brit. B.*, 51:41-56, 103-18.
COLLIER, R V (1970) *Birds of Inverpolly Nature Reserve* (privately circulated brochure).
CUNNINGHAM, W A J (1962) The Stornoway Woods, *Scot. B.*, 2:89-96.
DARLING, F F (1939) *A Naturalist on Rona*, Oxford.
DARLING, F and BOYD J M (1968) *The Highlands and Islands* (2nd ed.), London.
DIAMOND, A W *et al* (1965) Notes on the Birds of Berneray, Mingulay and Pabbay, *Scot. B.*, 3:397-404.
DUNNET, G M and ANDERSON, A (1963) A Study of Survival of Adult Fulmars . . ., *Brit. B.*, 561:2-18.
EVANS P R and FLOWER, W U (1967) The Birds of the Small Isles, *Scot. B.*, 4:404-45.
FAIR ISLE BIRD OBSERVATORY REPORTS (1968, 1969).
FISHER, J (1949) Natural History of Inverpolly Forest, *Bird Notes*, 23:253-60.
GILROY, N (1923) *Field-Notes and Observations on the Greenshank* (privately circulated brochure).
GOODFELLOW, P F (1961) The Birds of Corrour Forest, Inverness-shire, *Scot. Nat.*, 70:48-59.
GORDON, S (1927) *Days with the Golden Eagle*, London. (1953) *The Golden Eagle*, London.
HARVIE-BROWN, J A *et al* (1887-1904) *Vertebrate Fauna* series, Edinburgh.
HUNTER, E N (1970) Great-northern Diver Breeding in Scotland, *Scot. B.*, 6:195.
LOCKIE, J D and STEPHEN, D (1959) Eagles, Lambs and Land Management, *J. Anim. Ecol.*, 28:43-50.
LOCKLEY, R (1959) *in* Bannerman, D., 8:92-100.
MCGEOCH, J (1959) *in* Bannerman, D., 8:33-34.
MARTIN, M (1698) *A Late Voyage to St Kilda*, London.
MEIKLEJOHN, M F M and STANFORD, J K (1954) June Notes on the Birds of Islay, *Scot. Nat.*, 66: 129-45.
NETHERSOLE-THOMPSON, D (1951) *The Greenshank*, London. (1966) *The Snow Bunting*, Edinburgh and London. (1971) *The Dotterel*, London.
NETHERSOLE-THOMPSON, D and WATSON, A (1974) *The Cairngorms*, London.
PENNIE, I (1962) Bird-watching in Sutherland, *Scot. B.*, 2:167-92.
PETERSON, R *et al* (1958) *A Field Guide to the Birds of Britain and Europe*, London.
RATCLIFFE, D A (1969) *in Peregrine Falcon Populations*, Madison, Milwaukee and London.
ST JOHN, C (1884) *A Tour in Sutherlandshire*, 2 Vols. (2nd ed.), Edinburgh.
SAXBY, H L (1874) *The Birds of Shetland* . . ., Edinburgh.
SCOTTISH BIRDS, Vols. 1-6 (many notes and papers).
SELBY, P J (1836) On the Quadrupeds and Birds Inhabiting the County of Sutherland, *Edin. New. Phil. Jour.* for 1836: 156-61, 286-95.
SMITH, R W J (1969) Scottish Cormorant Colonies, *Scot. B.*, 5:363-78.
STARK, D M (1967) A Visit to Stack Skerry and Sule Skerry *Scot. B.*, 4:548-53.
TULLOCH, R J (1969) Snowy Owls Breeding in Shetland, *Scot. B.*, 5:244-57.
TULLOCH, R J and HUNTER, F (1970) *A Guide to Shetland Birds*, Lerwick.
VENABLES, L S V and U (1955) *Birds and Mammals of Shetland*, Edinburgh and London.
WATERSTON, G (1959) *in* Bannerman, D., 8:21-34.
WATERSTON, G and DENNIS, R (1973) *Ospreys and Speyside Wildlife* (R.S.P.B.).

Contents

Illustrations

Going North?

What makes the Highlands so special? In this huge expanse of mountain, moorland and romantic islands there are many exciting birds. Some you find only in the Highlands or you find them more often here than in any other part of Britain. Everyone knows of golden eagle, osprey and snowy owl. They have had The Treatment. The great sea cliffs with their enormous sea-bird 'cities', full of noise and beauty, are always a magnet. To these you shall return again and again. But only the spirited and adventurous will watch fork-tailed petrels nesting on wild St Kilda and North Rona.

On a few high bens, often deep in mist, dotterels run on twinkling legs and ptarmigan croak like monstrous frogs. In this stony wilderness you may also hear the flute-like song of the tiny snow bunting. Here are golden eagles on the cliffs and ring ouzels in the corries. In Speyside and some other forests, crested tits, Scottish crossbills and siskins are in the pines, and huge capercaillies and martial blackcocks lek in woods and clearings. On the grey flows of Sutherland the greenshank's song challenges the hunter and the weird music of divers forever haunts him. There, in lonely solitude, you listen to golden plovers in evening chorus and watch dunlins rise and fall as if controlled by invisible elastic. On lochs in softer country, close to Inverness, rare and colourful Slavonian grebes hold their penguin dances.

On almost endless summer days in Orkney you watch hen harriers hunting brown hills and little valleys, short-eared owls nesting in the heather, and merlins chattering overhead. On some Shetland islands whimbrels sing and contend with marauding bonxies and arctic skuas. These islands also hold huge gannetries and sea-bird colonies. You will sail to the Western Isles where there are communities of greylag geese and dainty hen red-necked phalaropes woo and win cocks. Islay still has its choughs and Rum its mountain shearwaters.

You are coming to the Highlands in brave days. In these last twenty years of cooling climate great northern diver, scaup, goldeneye, whooper swan, probably goshawk, marsh harrier, and spotted crake, black-tailed godwit, green sandpiper, Temminck's stint, fieldfare, bluethroat and brambling have all nested; and wood sandpiper, osprey, snowy owl and redwing are now well established in remote and sometimes secret places. In future who knows what you may find? Long-tailed duck, turnstone, dusky redshank, purple and broad-billed sandpiper, ruff, great grey shrike and pine grosbeak are all among the many exciting possibilities. Now waxwings have prospected and shorelarks probably nested.

As a boy, I had casually watched birds in Haute Savoie, the Bernese Oberland and the Dolomites and in Normandy and the Ardennes. As a young man, I had had a good innings—ravens and buzzards in Devon and Cornwall, peregrine, Dartford, marsh and grasshopper warblers in Sussex, hobby and woodlark in the Home Counties, honey buzzard in New Forest, stone curlew and crossbill in Breckland, bittern, bearded tit and Montagu's harrier in

Opposite: In these last twenty years of cooling climate, some boreal birds have started to nest in Scotland. Fieldfares have already nested in Orkney, Shetland, and on both sides of the Cairngorms. They are now quite well established on the Highland mainland.

Below: Redwing at the nest. Look out for these attractive northern thrushes, already established in several rather secret Highland places.

the Norfolk Broads, kite in south-central Wales, choughs in Antrim and black-necked grebes in Roscommon. I had known and successfully hunted them all. I was twenty-four before I went to the Highlands, but I had already read every word that the old naturalists had written and knew that I could never belong until I had met this challenge.

In 1932 I had saved enough from my miserly salary as a schoolmaster to go north. It was a grand investment! In the Spey Valley I found my first crested tit's nest and stayed with an ancient gamekeeper who had been guide to Harvie-Brown, F. C. Selous and John Millais. After my first night in his cottage I killed thirty-nine fleas! Then I trained it to Sutherland where James McNicol, an outstanding naturalist-keeper, showed me my first greenshank's nest. After hunting greenshanks on the flows of Strath Helmsdale I knew that I had lost the first round. Then I was off to Orkney where another remarkable self-taught naturalist took me to his heart. I never learnt so much as in those crowded weeks. In 1933 I was back north. I watched greenshanks in Rothiemurchus and dotterels in the Cairngorms. I was now completely hooked! The Highlands were the only place for me. In 1934 I was back for good. Perhaps I was the original Counterdrifter.

From the late eighteenth century onwards trophy-hunters harried the Highlands. A pretty bunch of villains they were—brash wealthy men, who sought the spectacular for their showcases. Prideaux C. Selby was a naturalist of great talent. His *Quadrupeds and Birds Inhabiting the County of Sutherland* (1836) has merit. Most of the rest were itchy-fingered, trigger-happy and mighty quick on the draw! In 1847 Sir William Milner, M.P., went to Sutherland where he looted nests of greylag geese, shot red-throated divers, greenshanks and hen harriers, and unsuccessfully pursued a black-throated diver. Afterwards he sailed to the Isles where he slew three pairs of red-necked phalaropes in North Uist. Charles St John, aristocrat, John Hancock, saddler and ironmonger, and Roualeyn Gordon-Cumming, poacher, African big game hunter and younger son of Moray Lairds, were great osprey killers, who loved Highland birds so much that their eggs and skins usually followed them home! The alcoholic naturalist extraordinary, Old Harrovian Edward T. Booth of Brighton, was a shocker. I have read his unpublished manuscript notebooks, where he describes in great detail how in the 1870's he did in the handful of red kites in the Spey Valley. All long ago perhaps? Yet I once knew an old gamekeeper in Rothiemurchus who helped to build the hide from which Booth shot a kite in Glenmore.

Modern bird-watchers and ornithologists are differently motivated. Bird-watching is now for all. As you grow older the hills seem steeper, but you still continue to learn. All that you need is the will. The great joy of bird-watching is that your wants are few and simple. You can make a start with notebook and biro or pencil, and a copy of Peterson's *Field Guide to the Birds of Britain and Europe.* A little later a good pair of field-glasses is a must. But shop around. For serious watching of nesting birds, a $7 \times$ or $8 \times$ glass, not too heavy and with a wide field, is best. For identifying waders or wildfowl on coast or estuary you need a $10 \times$, $12 \times$ or higher magnification, or perhaps a good telescope. For all the tea in China I would not part with my well-worn lightweight Zeiss Deltrintem, bought on skimped pounds in 1936. This has been my ally and good comrade ever since I bought it. The magnificent bloomed lenses of the 8×30B Zeiss, which I bought in 1961, are superior to those of my dear Deltrintem, but, to me, its performance is inferior. In moments of crisis I have often lost greenshanks and siskins when trying to follow them in flight. As you swing upwards with your glass a veiled shadow blocks out the field. I can prevent this by holding the joints of my first fingers between eyecups and spectacles or by raising the rubber eyecups in advance. But this greatly reduces the field of view. Five years ago we gave Bruin, our sixteen-year-old son, a pair of inexpensive 8×30 Nipole binoculars, as advertised in *Scottish Birds* and *Bird Life*. So successful have these been that we have bought pairs for Richard and Patrick.

I divide bird-watchers into two main groups—'leggers' and 'arsers'. Leggers move fast from 'good spot' to 'good spot', viewing and identifying. At a higher level they count birds and record their distribution. Many 'leggers', some quite young schoolboys, are fantastically skilful identifiers; but this meaningful sport and study has never really appealed to me. Legging seldom teaches you to understand your birds. Those who are prepared to sit for a few hours in one place are far more likely to discover how birds really tick. You do not need the patience of Job, but you must learn how to relax and concentrate. On quite mild spring days you will soon become stiff and cold, so take stout leather boots or gumboots, wear two pairs of socks and a couple of jerseys, gloves, overcoat and a warm hat. Even then you will sometimes find yourself too frozen to get to your feet! Some use snipers' capes and hoods, but these are seldom necessary as most birds behave quite naturally if you wait long enough and don't make sudden movements. Always raise and lower your arms and field-glasses slowly. You must also learn to know birds by their songs and calls and later how to interpret what you hear. This all takes time, but a whole new and exciting world will then gradually become yours. When you do become a real bird-watcher—no superhuman qualities are needed, believe me—wild horses won't drag you off the field. So, always take map, compass, torch and a substantial 'piece' in your bag, as you will seldom return in time for regular meals in Highland hotels.

Two bodies are particularly interested in Highland birds. The Scottish Ornithologists' Club, 21 Regent Terrace, Edinburgh, does a splendid job and publishes the quarterly *Scottish Birds* for which dedicated recorders sift and prepare field-notes and observations. The club has a fine library and runs an excellent bookshop.

The Royal Society for the Protection of Birds has its Scottish headquarters at 15 Regent Terrace, Edinburgh. The R.S.P.B. does much to conserve rare birds in the Highlands. You all know about their osprey hide at Boat of Garten. The Society also has fine Reserves on Handa Island in Sutherland and at Balranald in North Uist. Its Young Ornithologists' Club, to which three of my sons belong, publishes *Bird Life* and does much to interest young people. Do join these private and voluntary organisations before you go to Scotland.

The Nature Conservancy is the Government body responsible for research and conservation throughout Britain. Its Scottish headquarters are 12 Hope Terrace, Edinburgh and Dr John Morton Boyd is the Scottish Director. The Conservancy has important Nature Reserves in the Highlands, including the Cairngorms Reserve which is the largest of its kind in Europe. Other mainland reserves are Beinn Eighe and Inverpolly in Ross and Gualin in Sutherland. In the Hebrides, Rum, St Kilda and North Rona and in Shetland, Noss and Hermaness are particularly exciting Reserves for sea-bird communities. The Forestry Commission does much to help bird-watchers. In Glenmore Forest Park the Commission has built hides where, for a small fee, you can watch blackcock fighting at their leks. Do ask for the Commission's excellent brochures on wildlife whenever you visit a Forest Park.

We shall always associate the great Fair Isle project with Eagle Clarke, J. H. Stenhouse and George Waterston. Wardens Ken Williamson, Peter Davis and Roy Dennis have all given body and soul to this wonderful Observatory.

Raw to the Highlands in the 1930's, my vanity quickly took a knock. I had intended to watch the birds and quickly 'write them up'; but it has taken nearly forty years of intensive watching and research just to make a start. I have concentrated on a few birds, dotterel and snow bunting on the hill, greenshank and golden plover on flow and moor, and siskin, crested tit, and particularly Scottish crossbill in the forest. This has already led to *The Greenshank* (1951), *The Snow Bunting* (1966), *The Dotterel* (1973), and pioneer studies on eggshell disposal and nest-site selection. I am now writing *The Scottish Crossbill* and this year Adam Watson and I are publishing *The Cairngorms*.

In the 1950's peregrines started to break and eat their own eggs; breeding success was poor. Dr D. A. Ratcliffe (now Director of Research, Nature Conservancy), suspected that toxic-contaminated prey triggered off this behaviour. After reading an early draft of his paper I suggested that he weigh peregrine eggshells in an attempt to understand the nature of the egg-breaking phenomenon. Early results were dramatic. Eggshells taken after 1946, when DDT pesticides became prevalent, were significantly thinner and lighter. This hunch, which started in the Highlands, has led to British and North American ecologists developing the 'eggshell test', now a recognised research tool in assessing toxic-contamination in birds of prey.

While preparing this book I soon discovered how little we knew about Highland birds and how much there is still to do. In the late 1880's Harvie-Brown's famous *Vertebrate Faunas* laid the foundation of our distributional knowledge. Before the Second World War there was little kudos and still less money for naturalists in the Highlands. Seton Gordon was then one of the very few. For years his books inspired us all and he has probably forgotten more about golden eagles than any ever knew. His *Days with the Golden Eagle* and *The Golden Eagle* are classics. In the traumatic late 1930's and during the War, Fraser Darling worked and camped among grey seals in North Rona and studied the social life of sea-birds and other animals in the Highlands and Islands.

Since 1945 attitudes have changed. Many more scientists are working in the Highlands. In Orkney, Eddie Balfour, R.S.P.B., is doing fine research on hen harriers and in Spey Valley Nick Picozzi and D. N. Weir are studying the population dynamics of buzzards. Nature Conservancy ecologists are hard at work on Rum, St Kilda and other islands, and Jim Lockie has studied the golden eagle's ecology in Wester Ross and in other Highland places. Under Prof. G. Dunnet's direction Aberdeen University scientists are doing long-term professional research on fulmar petrels at Eynhallow in Orkney, and Dr Adam Watson's Unit of Moorland and Mountain Ecology at Banchory is intensively studying the behaviour and populations of red grouse and ptarmigan.

This is not enough. Ecologists and ornithologists have underestimated the potential of the Highlands and Islands as a natural field laboratory. We urgently need a Research Institute in the Highlands, with field stations in the islands and remoter places. The Highlands contain one-fifth of the land mass of Britain. In these years with so many increasing pressures, the Highlands and Islands Development Board is anxious to conserve as well as develop our precious resources.

Some Rare or Unusual Birds Recorded in the Highlands and Islands (1965-73)

Spey Valley
Red kite, goshawk, marsh harrier, hobby, gyr falcon, spotted crake and bluethroat.

East Inverness and Ross
Sooty shearwater, green-winged teal, American wigeon, smew, red kite, honey buzzard, crane, spotted crake, grey plover, grey phalarope, Temminck's stint, Iceland and Sabine's gulls, white-winged black tern, hoopoe and citrine wagtail.

West Inverness and Argyll
White stork, king eider, crane, ivory gull, Brünnich's guillemot, yellow-billed cuckoo, hoopoe, alpine swift, lesser grey shrike and red-headed bunting.

Inner Isles
Red-necked grebe (Skye), little egret (Mull), goshawk (Rum), snow goose, buff-breasted sandpiper (Islay), dowitcher (Tiree), ivory gull (Coll), roller (Islay), hoopoe (Eigg), Richard's pipit (Islay), lesser-grey shrike (Rum), golden oriole (Tiree and Iona), rose-coloured starling (Iona), black-headed bunting (Islay) and red-headed bunting (Rum).

Outer Isles
Great and Cory's shearwaters (Lewis), little egret (North Uist), spoonbill (Lewis), flamingo (South Uist and South Harris), scaup (Benbecula), Steller's eider (South Uist), snow goose, hobby and gyr falcon (Lewis), white-rumped sandpiper (Lewis), Baird's sandpiper (North Uist), Iceland gull (Benbecula and Lewis), little gull (St Kilda), white-winged black tern (Lewis), snowy owl (Lewis and St Kilda), hoopoe, golden oriole (Lewis), grey-cheeked thrush (St Kilda), red-headed bunting (St Kilda) and rustic bunting (South Uist).

Orkney
Sooty shearwater, black-browed albatross, white stork, black stork, snow goose, blue-winged teal, smew, goshawk, black kite, honey buzzard, gyr and red-footed falcon, crane, sociable plover, dowitcher white-rumped sandpiper, pectoral sandpiper, little gull, snowy owl, Scops owl, alpine swift, bee-eater, roller, bluethroat, icterine, melodious, barred, subalpine and yellow-browed warblers, firecrest, red-breasted flycatcher, Richard's pipit, lesser grey and woodchat shrikes, scarlet grosbeak, ortolan, black-headed, pine and rustic buntings, arctic redpoll and scarlet rosefinch.

Fair Isle
Sooty and Cory's shearwaters, purple heron, Steller's eider, honey buzzard, marsh harrier, osprey, hobby, gyr falcon, spotted crake, great bustard, little ringed and grey plovers, great snipe, pectoral sandpiper, buff-breasted sandpiper, upland sandpiper, collared pratincole, pomarine skua, Iceland and little gulls, gull-billed tern, alpine swift, woodlark, nightingale, bluethroat, bee-eater, short-toed lark, golden oriole, Pallas's, river, marsh, lanceolated, great reed, thick-billed, aquatic, melodious, icterine, booted, barred, subalpine, greenish, arctic, and yellow-browed warblers, red-breasted flycatcher, Richard's, tawny, Pechora and red-throated pipits, citrine wagtail, lesser grey and woodchat shrikes, rock thrush, White's thrush, rose-coloured starling, golden oriole, goldfinch, serin, scarlet rosefinch, scarlet grosbeak, two-barred crossbill, white-throated sparrow, black-headed, red-headed, yellow-breasted, ortolan, rustic and little buntings, and little crake and thrush nightingale.

Shetland
Great and sooty shearwaters, little bittern, great white egret, green-winged teal, king eider, goshawk, black kite, honey buzzard, marsh harrier, hobby, gyr and red-footed falcons, crane, spotted crake, marsh sandpiper, dowitcher, pomarine skua, ivory and Ross's gulls, black tern, Brünnich's guillemot, alpine swift, bee-eater, roller, short-toed lark, red-rumped swallow, golden oriole, nutcracker, dusky thrush, American robin, bluethroat, thick-billed, aquatic, icterine, barred, subalpine, arctic and yellow-browed warblers, firecrest, red-breasted flycatcher, nightingale, thrush nightingale, red-flanked bluetail, Richard's pipit, tawny pipit, Pechora pipit, black-headed wagtail, lesser grey and woodchat shrikes, slate-coloured junco, serin, scarlet rosefinch, two-barred crossbill, scarlet grosbeak, and black-headed, yellow-breasted, ortolan, little and rustic buntings and American ovenbird (first European record, 1973).

Caithness
White stork, harlequin duck, gyr falcon, crane, white-rumped and marsh sandpipers, grey phalarope, Iceland gull, white-winged black tern, hoopoe, bluethroat, black-eared wheatear and barred warbler.

Sutherland
Red-necked grebe, snow goose, king eider, red-footed falcon, red kite, spotted crake, grey plover, stilt sandpiper, Bonaparte's gull, crane, snowy owl, hoopoe, icterine warbler, trumpeter bullfinch and rose-coloured starling.

Note: This list does not include records of great grey shrikes and waxwings, birds of the forests of Northern Europe. Great grey shrikes are now annually reported from many parts of the Highlands and Islands and waxwings arrive in quite high numbers in their irruption years.

The Spey Valley

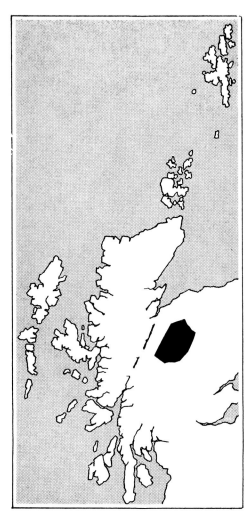

What a glorious challenge Spey Valley offers. Here are the rounded lumps of the Central Grampians, the grey mossy Monadhliath and the arctic wilderness of the high Cairngorms. In the valley are moors, lochs and rivers. The Insh Marshes, 'The Sponge of Badenoch', lost and water-logged farms, are among the finest wetlands in Scotland. There are also small tongues of almost boreal forest-bog. In Abernethy, Rothiemurchus and Glenmore, are relics of the old Caledonian Forest and many new pinewoods and conifer plantations; fascinating habitats for many birds.

From the 1950's onwards Spey Valley has often been in the news. Subtle climatic changes have probably induced many boreal birds to settle. Since 1954 ospreys have nested regularly; and goshawk and marsh harrier, bluethroat, pied flycatcher and wryneck, redwing, fieldfare and brambling, wood and green sandpiper have all nested or shown willing. Spotted crakes have also 'whiplashed' in the Insh Marshes and in July 1970 a duck goldeneye appeared with four ducklings on a forest lochan. There were two broods of goldeneyes in 1973.

If this southward drift of northern birds continues, these exciting colonists could all consolidate and perhaps others breed. We may yet see red kites and honey buzzards in the forests and great grey shrikes, broad-billed sandpipers and dusky redshanks in woodland marshes and forest fringes. In summer 1956 I watched a dusky redshank here.

But do not let us daydream. You will probably not go far into the forest before you hear a little purring trill. Just sit down or move towards the sound. On the bottle-green canopy of an old pine, a small grey bird with a curious little crest, white cheeks, and a black bib, is stuttering excitedly. This is the famous crested tit, a relic of post-glacial pine forests. This is May. That little bird is not far from its nest. Try to follow it through the trees; it may lead you a merry dance. At last, in a clearing, you see an old pine stump. Look at it and any others like it. At last you find a tiny jagged hole with a few deers' hairs sticking to it. Don't go away. Walk back about thirty yards and sit; you will soon have some fun. Every hour or so the cock crestie flies in, calls softly, and the little hen pops out of the hole and flies away with him. Or, perhaps, he *chirrs* softly, lands at the hole, depresses his crest, and goes in. You notice a small moth or some insects in his beak. A few seconds later he is out and flying silently through the trees. Almost every pair has a slightly different brooding rhythm. Describe all that you see in your notebook.

Come back later when chicks are in the nest. The little crested tits now ignore you. Watch these little gems foraging in the pines. See the hen flutter her wings like a young bird and hear her creaking cries as she signals to the cock to feed her. Then watch both, beaks crammed, go to feed their chicks. For you, time now stands still.

But we cannot all go to Spey Valley in lovely May. You are here in February or March, often sunny months here. Walk through the pines. Up above you hear a crackling and cones

The crested tit. Look at this little gem, its beak crammed with food for the chicks. In autumn 1973 they appeared in Deeside forests.

come plopping down. Look up! Seed cases are floating and parachuting; and in the foliage you hear the rustle of strong, leathery wings. That is all. Then, suddenly, screeching and claw to claw, two small birds go fluttering through the branches. Stand and watch. A mating party of Scottish parrot crossbills is just overhead. How tame they are. See them snip off the cones and extract the seeds with their strong crossed beaks. Did you ever see more lovely birds? Look at that cock in his scarlet guardsman's tunic! How different is that green hen with her bright yellow rump-patch. But how perfect the camouflage is against the gold and green pines. You see the crossbills and then you lose them, but always cones crackle and wings rustle. Don't go away. Watch the crossbills courting. See that lovely cock feed a hen. Watch her open her beak and quiver her wings as she invites his gift. But there goes a rival! The two cocks screech and grapple. They fight and fight and fight again before pairs are firm. You will love every moment.

You have just seen something very special. These parrot crossbills, like the crested tits, are relict birds. Although they sometimes mingle with flocks of visiting common crossbills, from the spruce forests of Fenno-Scandia, they remain apart and do not interbreed. These Scottish birds, with their slightly larger and more powerful bills, largely feed on pine cones, but common crossbills prefer the softer spruce. These fine Scottish birds also have a diagnostic call which helps to separate them from others of the crossbill kind.

A fortnight later, perhaps, you hear a metallic *chip* high in air and watch a stout little bird lilting over the wood. Follow his line and wait. Then, a few hours later, if your luck is in, you may watch a fine scarlet cock crossbill land on a pine top. Listen to his deep angry calls as he flirts his wings and flies from tree to tree. But he is quiet at last. Now he flies across the clearing, lands on a tree top, calls, and flirts his wings again; then at last he goes rustling down the branches. See! There is the nest—that little lump out on a lateral branch. Listen! Hear the sitting hen chittering like a mouse and watch her raise her head and shake her wings. The cock flutters through the branches and, standing on the nest, thrusts his beak in hers. Gulp after gulp of pine seeds he gives her, then he is up, off, and flying over the forest.

On forest-edge or in roadside stands of spruce and larch, you find siskins; small and lovely little finches. How dapper that cock siskin is. Look at his black bib and bonnet, green mantle and rump of yellow-green. There is the hen, streaky, less colourful, and without his black bib and bonnet. In autumn and early spring siskins haunt alders beside burns and rivers. But seek them in pines, larch or spruce when they are nesting.

Almost children of the sun, siskins come alive on warm days. Then, several cocks, slowly beating their wings and spreading their tails, sing in erratic bat-like flights. A fleeting glimpse of sunshine often stimulates joy-flights and jerky hurdy-gurdy songs. Then, just as suddenly, off they bound, their sad little cries growing fainter and fainter on the wind.

For nesters the siskin is a 'blue riband' bird. You will do well to best it. Flying fast and twisting through the upper branches, the cock dives through the forest and within seconds has fed the little hen on an almost invisible nest. Then, off he bounds again. For a few seconds the wood rang with soft mournful cries; but you failed to locate them. You wait, watch, and fail, but do persevere. At last you see the tiny nest at the end of a thin swaying branch. See, there is the hen's head and tiny forked fishtail as the cock bends down to feed her.

Strathspey forests have many other small birds. Goldcrests, coal tits and chaffinches in the pines, wood warblers and now sometimes pied flycatchers and redwings in broad-leaved woods, and tree pipits in the clearings. Not all rare birds, perhaps, but always beautiful and exciting. For every bird is unique and a thing of joy and wonder. Look at that cock redstart trying to lure a hen to that old grey stump over there. Time after time he pokes his head into that hole and spreads and shivers his fiery red tail, or he peeps out of it, flashing his white frontal patch. Is there a more lovely bird anywhere?

You now leave the forest fringe and flounder through long heather or walk over a green blaeberry carpet. Suddenly a huge black bird, like a turkey cock, rises, flaps, and crashes through the trees. That was a cock capercaillie, largest and most exciting of all our game birds. What sharp senses these capers have! Almost always they see or hear you first. These great cock capers have tremendous spring displays. But to watch them you must rise early in the morning. Surely that is a small price to pay? In late March or early April, then, you are out about an hour before dawn. Now listen for faint and distant clicking and sneezing noises; but do tread carefully and walk slowly. The sounds are louder. Is this some madman's orgy? Are those really corks popping from champagne bottles? You stalk from tree to tree. The pops and clicks are louder; but you stumble in the shadows. Strong wings wuffle and crash against branches. Go back. You've had it for today! But you must come back again. You sit in a heavy coat, gloved, scarved and jerseyed, hardly daring to move. There, on the forest path, are the caper cocks, with their throat feathers erect like those of angry ravens. See them droop their wings and spread their tails, almost vertically above their backs. Listen to the weird fantastic music. Perhaps the day may come when you will see a cock mating with a hen. Then you *will* belong.

In forest clearings and on some old crofts, black grouse also have leks. You really must watch a lek which, in early morning and late evening, is alive with colour and passion. You usually hear the blackcocks fighting long before you see them; but I was very lucky. Black-cocks met in a humpy field beside my cottage; I watched them from my window! Each cock had a small territory, a few square yards or so. On these stances the cocks stand, loose-winged, red wattles engorged, throats swollen, and feathers raised. They also hold up

Opposite: Cock dotterel brooding. 'You will know these little beauties by their tameness and bright colours'. The dotterel, a bird of the remote high tops, has a fascinating reversed courtship.

Below left: 'Rarest and most elusive hill bird is the snow bunting. A few cocks we came to know almost as people.'

Below right: Hardiest of all our native birds, ptarmigan have haunted the desolate barrens ever since the last Ice Age.

Left: Look how tenderly the great golden eagle feeds its chick.

Centre: The Loch Garten ospreys. This is what you may see from the R.S.P.B. hide, where many thousands of visitors have watched these exciting birds.

Right: Young osprey in the nest. In the 1950's ospreys returned to traditional haunts in the Spey Valley and have been nesting since 1954.

Left: Hen capercaillie brooding eggs. Our largest gamebird lays a clutch of five to eight eggs among heather, blaeberries or juniper scrub on the forest floor.

Right: The cock capercaillie's aggressive turkey-cock display. 'Their tail feathers almost vertical and their throat feathers erect like those of angry ravens.'

Left: The Cairngorms and Rothiemurchus Forest. The high tops are the haunt of dotterel, snow bunting and ptarmigan, and the forest holds Scottish crossbill, crested tit, siskin, capercaillie and sometimes nesting ospreys. Much of Rothiemurchus Forest is a National Nature Reserve.

Right: Woodcock settling down on eggs. 'Good observers have seen woodcocks carry their chicks, but although I have lived so long in woodcock country I have never seen them do this. Perhaps you will be luckier than I.'

22

Left: Beinn Dearg, west-central Ross. Only the strong and hardy can enjoy the high corries and ridges where the hill birds nest.

Centre: Immature golden eagle drops on prey in Beinn Eighe Nature Reserve.

Right: Peregrine falcon and young. In the 1950's prey contaminated by DDT pesticides caused peregrines to break and eat their own thinner-shelled eggs. Central Highland populations, feeding on local birds, almost alone escaped contamination.

Two blackcocks at lek. "The cock stands, loose-winged, red wattles engorged, throat swollen and feathers raised. They also hold up lyre-shaped tails to display white coverts."

lyre-shaped tails to display white coverts. In this savage ritual dance, cocks leap into the air or threaten and rush at one another. It is all very exciting. Sometimes one cock hits another with his wings; or he pecks at his rival's crown. At first the greyhens (as female black grouse are called) watch the dance from trees or at the edge of the lek and ignore the fighting cocks. Then, one day, when she is coming into season, the greyhen explores the lek. Now, as she walks slowly forward, pausing and stopping, each cock displays to her as she passes through his stance. Head and neck pushed forward, he tilts towards her or half-circles round her. See! He walks with quick steps, swinging his tail towards her. Or, there, he lies down with wings outstretched. The greyhen often passes several dancers before she stops. Then he possesses her. At other times she walks right through the lek or suddenly flies away without offering herself to any. Large leks have master cocks whose stances are often near the centre. These enjoy most of the greyhens.

The lochs and forest-bogs of Spey Valley are most exciting places. Here, in 1934 and 1936, Temminck's stints nested for the first time in Britain. In 1956 I found another nest. So small is this boreal wader, that it looks little larger than a dunlin chick. From 1933 onwards, we also often watched green sandpipers flying and song-dancing above the forest. But not until 1959 did two visiting ornithologists find a pair with chicks. In 1960 we also watched a pair and saw one green sandpiper fly into a big wood where it probably exchanged with its sitting mate. But we never found the nest. In all Britain I know of no greater prize than a green sandpiper's nest with eggs. Unlike other waders, these wonderful waders lay in the old nests of mistle or song thrush or in that of some other woodland bird, or even, perhaps, in a squirrel's drey. My heart beats fast at the thought of this elusive wader's nest!

Wood sandpipers, with their rich and lovely songs, have already nested. Small to middling-sized waders, of the greenshank kind, their legs jut out beyond their tails in flight. This is another thrilling bird. A local ornithologist has already handled a chick, but the first Speyside nest is still to come. I should love to have a go!

There are fewer greenshanks than when I used to watch them in the 1930's and 1940's. Admittedly these groups have always ebbed and flowed; we hope to discover why this is so. But my happy hunting grounds on the braes west of Loch Morlich are now shamefully bulldozed and completely destroyed for greenshanks. How did conservation policy break down?

Beside still and running waters in early May, graceful common sandpipers teeter and display. Without them loch and river could never be the same. On fields, water meadows, and on river shingle, are many groups of lapwings and oystercatchers. These fine birds also nest on many moors and farms. Few golden plovers now nest in the forest-marshes, but they still haunt moorland braes. A few ringed plovers nest on river shingle, but redshanks are scarce on the higher moors.

There are many better duck haunts than Strathspey, but there is always plenty to watch. In early spring goldeneyes court on many lochs. They have now nested and will doubtless nest again. I always love to watch mallards in the spring. Their 'threesome' chases are exciting. Teal are in the wetlands; on soft summer evenings their musical *crick cricks* are evocative. I always associate the drake wigeon's whistle with the happy days of the greenshank's homecoming. How lovely the drake is, with his chestnut head and buff-white topknot. The scarce grey-looking gadwall occasionally nests. I have found a nest and broods. Drake and duck have white specula, best seen on the wing. A few mergansers nest in shallow burrows or in rank herbage on river islands. Goosanders lay their big creamy eggs in hollow pines and alders, usually close to loch and burn. Watch the drake court a duck; see him bow stiffly, toss his head, and excitedly raise crown feathers; or watch him, beak to breast, stand up on the water.

From the Great North Road the Central Highland hills look less finely-etched and formidable than the wild bens of Wester Ross, the lone hills of Sutherland, or the black and red Cuillin of Skye. You have to live on them before you really understand their subtle charm and beauty. But there is really nothing in Britain quite like these huge windswept tablelands. Climb on to the long ridges above Drumochter or to the mossy bumps of Gaick. You will return and return until their gentle slopes become too steep. Search the crags and cliffs of the Monadhliath and Laggan hills where golden eagles, peregrines and ravens nest. Here I first heard the rare mewing squeal of an eagle when a raven was mobbing it.

The high Grampians and Cairngorms have special birds. In mid-winter skiers often see white grouse-like birds running almost beside them. Look with wonder. For these are ptarmigan, hardiest of all our native birds, which have haunted these desolate barrens ever since the last ice-age. How beautiful these ptarmigan are in winter; all white, except for red wattles and black eye-patches and tail feathers. In late March and early April, watch the ptarmigan groups dispersing. Now the pure white winter feather is almost gone. Cock and hen are moulting into grey birds, but the cock still has a white breast and his white wings show in his display flights. On mild spring days the hills are sometimes alive with ptarmigan. Head and red comb up, the cock struts after the hen, sometimes drooping his wings and fanning out his tail. On the borders of territories, cocks fight and challenge; only the dominant and aggressive win hens. Time after time the cock flies up, sings his belching song, and glides down on set wings. What raucous croaks you hear on these fine spring days! But there is still much more for you to see. In early May watch the hen crouch and the cock seize her crown feathers while he takes her. Or, as you toil up a stony flank, see that grey hen flop and flounder from her nest. You now need no field-glasses. All around you she runs, crouches, hisses. There the cock flies in. Head up, tail spread, 'crackling' noisily, he tries to chase her back to eggs.

On a few high ridges or stony broadbacks look out for dotterels. You will know these little beauties by their tameness and bright colours. See their dark brown crowns, dove-grey necks and broad white eyestripes and breastbands. Mark those red-brown lower breasts and flanks and the great ink-black belly patches. The larger, brighter hen dominates in the small mating groups. She woos and wins a mate and later leaves him with her eggs. Then she, and other 'grass widows', form wandering trips which spar and fight but seldom visit their hard-worked mates. A few hens take two mates; one, the famous *Blackie*, put her first mate down on three eggs, and then about ten days later produced three more eggs for a second cock. She then helped her second mate to brood the eggs. *Blackie* was quite a dotterel! In 1920 a fine Scottish naturalist, George Blackwood first suspected, but could not prove, that dotterels were sometimes polyandrous. How thrilled we were to prove this in 1934. For over thirty years I have tried to understand what makes dotterels tick. They do better on the richer carpets of some east Grampian hills where there is usually a ratio of one flying young to every old bird. But on the Cairngorm barrens the ratio is often one to five.

Rarest and most elusive hill bird is the snow bunting; a small bird about the size of a house sparrow. Many search but few ever find nests in Scotland. It took us over 250 nights in small tents to find thirty-eight nests. How I love the song-flights of those lovely piebald cocks in the smoky mist of rough corries. A few snow buntings we came to know almost as people. The cocks we knew by the distinctive plumage and the hens by their eggs. Some memories are precious. There was *Baldy*, the eager seducer, who never won a hen. *Romeo*, the great lover, once had three wives. His first two hens had nests about 150 yards apart, but this was not enough. He won the wife of another cock; I actually saw him take her. I love to watch these cock snow birds courting hens. With half-drooped wings and spread tails, they run away to show off jet-black mantles, white wings, and outer tail-feathers. No Parisienne mannequin does better!

There is probably no permanent stock of Scottish snow buntings. Decades of severe winters in Iceland, Scandinavia or possibly farther north, together with hard years and plenty of suitable snow on the Highland hills, may induce a handful of wintering snow birds to settle and thus establish, maintain or resurrect small nesting groups. We now know that Iceland cocks have dark rumps and those from Scandinavia and the north have pure white rump patches. Cocks with both white and dark rumps sometimes nest on the same hill in the same year. So, whenever you are close to a cock snow bird in summer, do note the colour of its rump-patch. Help us to advance an exciting story.

In winter thousands of immigrant snow buntings visit Scotland, where they feed on stack and stubble. When they rise together, turning and swerving in the sunshine, they look like a flurry of snowflakes—that is what the Highlanders often call them. 'Snowflakes' also feed on scraps. You will see them close to chairlift stations on Cairngorm and beside the Ptarmigan Restaurant.

A few other birds also haunt the tops in summer. On the Gaick and Drumochter hills and on the Big Moss in the West Cairngorms are dunlins and golden plovers. In some years black-faced cock goldies, with pure white eye and neck stripes, indistinguishable from northern cocks, sometimes breed here. You will know the cock dunlin by his tameness, strident pea-whistle song and yo-yo flights. In high corries wheatears *chack* on rocks and cock ring ouzels pipe from rowan trees. Meadow pipits nest in gullies and montane grass-lands and skylarks sing over Grampian tops and western Cairngorms. Common and black-headed gulls have also nested on islets on a high tarn. In the high country you may also watch an eagle soaring or a peregrine winnowing across a corrie; or, perhaps, even spot a snowy owl, looking just like a child's snowman.

You see golden eagles less often in the Cairngorms than in the western Highlands. But there are enough pairs and eyries here to test wind, legs and powers of observation. One early morning I crept up to an eagle's eyrie in a pine and saw the hen with dew drops glistening on her head. Some Cairngorm eagles hunt geese. Probably every autumn they gather like the Red Baron's circus over the flightlines of the skeins. I have seen eagles chasing geese, but Brock saw one cut down a greylag above Glen Einich. The eagle singled out the goose and beat and drove its wings until it had caught it up and struck it down.

Central Highland peregrines are a group of special interest. They have avoided toxic contamination better than any peregrines in Britain. In 1964-65 D. A. Ratcliffe found:

Region	Possible total eyries	Occupied eyries	Successful eyries	Yg. per occ. eyrie	Yg. per succ. eyrie
Wales	100	34	8	0·5	2·0
Northern England	85	46	10	0·3	1·5
Southern Scotland	55	46	12	0·4	1·7
Central Highlands	50	49	43	2·2	2·5

These peregrines had evidently found enough local birds to feed on throughout the year and had thus avoided taking poisoned pigeons elsewhere.

A few merlins chatter and gallop high over heathery braes where the hen will later lay her red darkly-speckled eggs. Some use old hoodies' nests high up in pines. I once found two tree nests in the same year.

In the 1920's and 1930's I knew of only one pair of buzzards nesting on a western Cairngorm flank, but they now mew over many woods and rocks. In 1969 the researchers counted thirty-three breeding pairs on the valley floor between Kingussie and Boat of Garten. Among many interesting discoveries they have found that a few cocks had two hens.

These great woods have other raptors. Kestrels avoid the depths of the old forest but sparrowhawks still do well. In 1968 they reckoned that there was one pair to 1000 acres in these Speyside woods. There are other possibilities. A few goshawks nested until the early 1850's. In 1877 the Glenmore keepers showed Booth the tree where the last native goshawk had nested about twenty-five years before. Now these magnificent hawks are coming back. In 1959 I watched a cock sparrowhawk flying with a hen goshawk—an almost incredible contrast in size. Then, in 1960, I watched a pair in April and in late July heard a gos chatter in anger and saw three goshawks flying through the trees.

I suppose that every bird-watcher has some secret ambition. Mine used to be the osprey. Long before I lived in the Highlands I had read all about these wonderful birds which had probably last nested in Britain in 1908; the year that I was born. A big hawk, $5\frac{1}{2}$ feet across the wing, deep brown above, a snowy-white breast and a white head, how I longed to find the nest. And the eggs, I also knew, were right out of this world!—big eggs, two or three of them, of creamy-ground colour, almost completely covered with great blood-red blotches and violet undermarkings. In the early 1950's my ambition came true. I well remember those James Bond days of the osprey's homecoming. Brock first tracked down a brood in 1954. I can still see the pair which nested in 1956 in Rothiemurchus Forest. Through a telescope I often watched these lovely birds from my window. What a thrill it was to see them change over at the nest. Sometimes they had a greeting rite; at others the cock stood on the nest until the hen rose and slowly flapped off to her feeding tree. I have also seen him hover over the eyrie with fish in talons and then drop down to it. Then the hen some-times rose; and the two ospreys faced one another beating their wings. While the hen was brooding, the cock brought sticks and built a rough platform round the nest; and the hen raised her white head to look at him as he balanced beside her. Once I saw him chase a harmless wood pigeon as well as the hoodies which were always annoying him. In another year I saw two ospreys fighting before one peeled off and glided to a second nest.

The ospreys had a curious way of building. One would fly to an old pine, and then with flaps of its great wings hang or hover over a dead stick which it broke off without alighting. On a still day I could hear the sharp crack as the stick snapped. Several times I watched the ospreys mating on a stump or on the edge of the nest. But once I saw them come together in the air. That was one of the most lovely sights I have ever seen. The balance and wing control of the two big hawks was something of truly wondrous beauty.

30

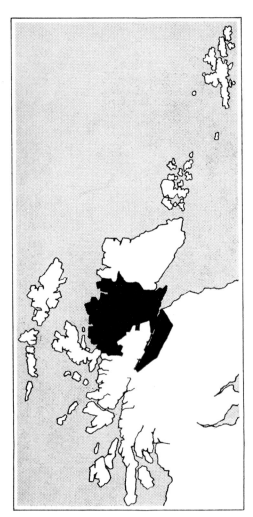

Between Carrbridge and Inverness are small rolling hills, flats and heathery braes. This is not the most exciting bird country in the Highlands, but there is plenty for those who look around. Forest-bogs north of Carrbridge can be rewarding. Greenshanks nested here and probably still do so. There are many excellent habitats here. Even if you only watch red grouse becking or hear curlews bubbling you will have had a good day. Crossbills sometimes nest in scattered trees in these forest-marshes. Peregrines also nest in a small crag close to the Great North Road. While watching here look for buzzards soaring over the woods and moors.

Few naturalists use the road and tracks which go far into the Monadhliath. Climb to the high grasslands where golden plovers call and dotterels nest. Few really know these hills and their golden eagles. I knew one eyrie to which a child could walk.

For over sixty years beautiful Slavonian grebes have nested on grassy lochs above Inverness. Why not look at them? No birds are more lovely and confiding. Look at their red-brown necks and upper breasts and their gorgeous titian red-gold head tufts and cold red-currant eyes. Sit on the bank and watch them in all their glory. See that pair courting on the water outside a sedgy bay. There the cock swims round the hen, stretching his neck and raising his red-gold horns. Now he bows to her and jerks his head from left to right or right to left. Or watch them build their floating nest of rotting water weeds. First one, then the other, swims in with weeds in its beak. Sit quiet and they will ignore you. Now watch them mating. The hen crouches on the nest, stretching out her neck, and the cock swims in and out, bowing up to her. Round and round he swims and then at last he jumps up on to her back. For weeks you watch these grebes and every day you learn. See them in their penguin dance! Almost standing on their tails in the water, cock and hen face one another, stretching forward, shaking heads, and always squeaking. Later watch cock and hen change guard at the nest and listen to their clamour. I watched a pair exchange every four to five hours, but you will find that almost all these lovely pairs have different rhythms and rituals. Is there anything more lovely than to see a grebe cover its eggs with weeds before it leaves its nest and swims away? Dab-dab with its beak and the white or brown-stained eggs are almost hidden. Just look at that nest and three eggs shown on the cover. One egg is pure white and freshly-laid, the two others are already slightly discoloured because the nest is made of rotting weeds.

Why not intensively study these grebes throughout late spring and summer? No one has yet really done them justice. Before the First World War, Julian Huxley watched great crested grebes and K. L. Simmons has carried on his work. You can easily learn as much about Slavonian grebes and do your work in a much more dramatic setting. Each pair of grebes has character of its own; and all subtly differ from their neighbours. Before long you will be calling *your* birds by pet names—then you will have arrived.

When the cock parrot crossbill arrives to feed her, the hen raises her head and shivers her wings in an agony of supplication. Our relict crossbills are now much scarcer in the northern Highlands, but common crossbills from the continent are now nesting in new plantations in Argyll and Perth.

In this big country of hill and crag and loch and moor there are many other exciting birds. Black-throated divers often nest here. Watch that pair swimming together and listen to their wails and growls. See the cock chase the hen in high courtship flight. Round and round they fly, now small specks known only by their distinctive flight and fast-driven wings. Then watch them on the water. The hen rolls over, showing white flanks to excite the cock. You will have few dull moments with the black-throats; and we still await a complete life-history study from a Highland loch.

Here, not long ago, we listened to the wailing of eyass peregrines on a crag. Then, in the evening, we saw tiercel, falcon, and flying young, and heard the unforgettable angry raucous scream. Buzzards soared over woods and kestrels hovered above moors. In late afternoon an osprey plunged almost beside a boat and flew away with a trout towards a distant hill. Behind it were a noisy mob of screaming common gulls. Who knows what you will find if you really work and search these hills?

In scrubland and around wood edges whinchats sing and redstarts flirt crimson tails. Redwings have also nested in the straths. It is up to you to find them. On a few stony moors greenshanks are still nesting in haunts where Macomb Chance found them over sixty years ago.

In the evening stroll through the birches. Suddenly a dark-looking bird, with a longish beak, flies overhead on quite fast almost owl-like wings. It calls a thin, loud, *tzik-tzik*, almost like a flying pied wagtail. Now and then it hesitates, almost hovers, and utters throaty croaks. This is the famous 'roding' flight of the woodcock. Now sit down, if the midges will allow you! The woodcock will soon pass by again, often flying about five and twenty feet above the trees. Stay long enough and you will hear shrill excited *zip-zips* and see your woodcock pursue another. Soon the cock has cleared his lines and is on patrol again. Why not make this strange woodcock one of your special birds? Good observers have seen woodcocks carry their chicks, but although I have lived so long in woodcock country I have never seen them do this. I have only watched the hen's distraction display; she flaps off low over the birchwood carpet with quickly beating wings and downspread tail. This can easily deceive you, but some hens really do carry off their young. Perhaps, then, you will be luckier than I. This is only one woodcock problem. We know little about its breeding behaviour; but in the 1930's I spent many chilly early mornings and late evenings watching nesting woodcocks. Are woodcocks polyandrous or polygamous? Do pairs part after mating? Does the hen join the cock in the 'roding' flight? At dawn or dusk do cocks call hens off or visit them when they are brooding? How long does the hen brood before the eggs hatch? How does she rear her chicks? Where do the cocks go? How do they behave in the late breeding season? Are woodcocks regularly double-brooded? In the gloaming

does the hen really carry her chicks from woods to marshes? I know some of the answers,
but you will learn much more than I ever knew.

We all seek the rare, exotic or unusual. But the common and expected are often just as exciting. I have watched herring gulls courting and mating on the ballroom roof of the old Caledonian Hotel in Inverness. Tossing her head and crying softly, a hen circled her mate, who stretched forward with open beak and swollen neck. He then spewed up a nauseating mess for her. Meanwhile, the excited hen pushed her beak between his mandibles and started to eat his love gift! I saw another pair here, tossing their heads and walking round one another. Suddenly the cock stretched up his neck and gave his raucous copulation calls. Then, flapping his wings, he jumped onto the hen's back. Meanwhile, she continued to jerk her head from side to side and rub her beak against his breast. After the well-satisfied cock had shuffled off her back, the hen pecked at the ground, waggled her tail and preened. All this, as a free cabaret, for the fascinated diners of the Permissive Society.

Herring gulls did not then breed in Inverness, but for a few years brave pairs have now nested on high buildings. One angry gull dive-bombed a nervous steeplejack; and the County Chief Constable had the bird shot!

The River Ness is another bird haunt. Watch those dippers with fish fry in their beaks. I have seldom seen them catch fry on wilder hill burns. Bobbing on stones or flying fast above the flood, these black-and-white and golden-brown water ouzels are truly lovely birds. Woods, gardens and shrubberies all have their birds. Collared doves are nesting. Here song thrushes, blackbirds and robins, blue and great tits, greenfinches, chaffinches and hedge sparrows all have territories. Never forget that we now probably know more about dotterels and golden eagles than about those homely but secretive hedge sparrows.

Few professional ornithologists have ever seen a cock blackbird court his hen. Have you? Watch him erect his rump feathers and then spread and droop his tail as he slowly creeps towards her. Has anyone watched house sparrows in Inverness? Most ignore them because they are so familiar. Yet no other British bird has a more exciting sex-life. Seen close by and in good light, starlings have real beauty. Can you tell me if cock starlings here have several wives or are they just conformists?

Stop beside Loch Ness, count the scrubland birds, measure distances between singing cocks, particularly tits and chaffinches. Look for little breeding groups of lesser redpolls. How dainty those pied wagtails are. See two cocks pursue a hen in bouncing, bounding flight. Watch that cock on the shore, crouching and crawling round his mate. Look how he throws back his head to show off his jet-black gorget. There he zig-zags up to her, bowing and flutter-jumping. Or, he spreads his wings and lowers and erects his tail. Now he raises his

"For nesters the siskin is a blue riband bird." Many hundreds nest in conifer woods in East Inverness and Ross. They are now also nesting in Rum and in Skye.

34

rump feathers like a courting blackbird. Watch him flutter and hover before he drops on to her back where, fastly beating his wings, he mates her.

Above pines growing from the crags, buzzards soar and mew. Watch them spar with hoodie crows. Rolling over on their backs they thrust upwards with stumpy legs if the crows become too cheeky. On both sides of Loch Ness the credulous are for ever seeing 'golden eagles' sitting on telegraph poles!

Why not drive over Glenconvinth and back to Inverness. You should find the small hill loch where Slavonian grebes often nest. In woods around the town sparrowhawks wicker to their young and siskins joy-fly over larches. Somewhere, in not too distant birches, red-wings are also nesting.

Southern bird-watchers know Strathspey and have heard of Wester Ross and Sutherland, but they seldom visit hills and straths in north Inverness and Easter Ross. Is this because these fine haunts are only reached by minor roads and tracks? The Victorians knew Glen Affric and Glen Strathfarrar. Booth took ospreys and golden eagles there, sent 'foresters' to scout for snow buntings on Sgurr na Lapaich and hunted siskins close to Erchless Castle. Before Glen Strathfarrar was flooded for a hydro-electric scheme, it was grand greenshank country. Here, on Monar Forest, the famous birdsnesting laird sent out his stalkers with their telescopes to track down greenshanks on nestward flights. In 1947, in a remote glen, a cock wood sandpiper sang over a forest bog. Dotterels also sometimes nest on these rounded hills. Search, watch, and find.

On rich farmlands along the Cromarty Firth are small groups of corn buntings. These greatly suffered during the severe winter of 1962-63 and have never recovered. Many lapwings nest on these fertile farms; but I wonder whether their groups contain as many eager adulterers and adulteresses as those I knew on the Braes of Abernethy.

Easter Ross holds some wonderful mixed woods. These now harbour fewer parrot crossbills than in the early 1900's, but I am never idle. For many years crossbills and crested tits have nested in one small crow-sown woods. In larger pinewoods parrot crossbills and siskins nest in higher numbers, but crested tits are scarce. Here buzzards, sparrowhawks and kestrels all nest and magpies are multiplying. The rare honey buzzards formerly nested. In these years of change watch for them. Great spotted woodpeckers and a few long-eared owls are in some larger woods. Capercaillies and blackcocks have leks. Coal tits dominate in the pines, great and blue tits in oak, birch and beech. On scrubby edges you find yellowhammers, lesser redpolls and long-tailed tits. Grasshopper warblers reel in several young plantations; wrynecks are prospecting; and redwings continue to colonise. Look for bramblings in the birches.

A pair of charming crested tits near their nest in an old pine-stump. A few crested tits nest in Easter Ross almost up to the Sutherland border.

On streams and rivers are dippers, some grey wagtails, and many common sandpipers. On 25th April 1970, an ex-Lord Lieutenant's butler discovered kingfishers nesting in a river bank about two feet above the water. Daily he watched and meticulously recorded them, hooking out and carefully replacing each egg as it was laid. On 30th May all six eggs had hatched, but a summer spate washed out the brood. How wonderful to find a fellow bird-watcher with such interest and gentle hands.

On moorlands and in new forests hen harriers and short-eared owls are nesting; no need now to travel to Orkney or the Hebrides. On other moors and grass-heaths are golden plovers and red grouse, snipe in boggy hollows, and groups of redshanks in grassy wetlands. Here merlins hunt meadow pipits and occasional wheatears and peregrines and ravens haunt quite small crags which few ever search.

Farther back are higher hills. The broad plateau of Ben Wyvis contains one of the finest moss-heaths in Scotland. On this whaleback early in the century, F. C. Selous, lion-hunter and African explorer, found his first dotterel's and ptarmigan's nests. A few others have since found dotterels here, but less frequently than I should have expected. There are dunlins on the flats, ring ouzels, wheatears and occasionally snow buntings in the roughest corries, and golden eagles on the crags. Better golden eagle habitats lie a little farther west. In the nineteenth century ospreys nested on larger lochs in this wild country. But we still await firm breeding records. Whooper swans have also nested.

The north coast of Inverness and Easter Ross is flat and cliffless, but many lapwings and oystercatchers nest on the shores and saltings. Here and there are small groups of ringed plovers and shelducks; and in an unexpected tongue of forest marsh among farmlands, a few pairs of black-headed gulls are in community. By building a causeway across a bay, railway engineers created an artificial haunt for waterfowl. You can watch them from your carriage window. But Easter Ross holds still more exciting birds. A few pairs of whimbrels now nest regularly in strange habitats. In 1971 Chris Headlam photographed Temminck's stints and chicks on marshy ground close to a river mouth. These tiny waders were back in 1973. Barn owls and nightjars are nesting here.

Few work this coast for breeding birds, but careful combing of unromantic country some-times does pay off. In 1970 friends found nearly 100 pairs of sandwich terns nesting on dunes where they formerly bred in the 1930's. Need I elaborate?

Cross to the Black Isle and find entirely different country with contrasting habitat-mosaics. In farmland with old-fashioned hedges, yellowhammers, song and mistle thrushes, black-birds, dunnocks, robins and wrens all join the dawn chorus in early spring. In May white-throats are on the wires, willow warblers trill in thickets, and a few chiffchaffs sometimes nest. Do look and listen for bramblings and redwings in the birches. Some small bogs and

swamps still remain. In some of these shovellers and pintails formerly nested and may still do so. All these swamps are well worth exploring. Crossbills sometimes feed on the older pines, siskins on larch and spruce, and redpolls on birches. On tilled fields and grasslands, cock lapwings make wing music, and seapies trill on shore and farm. Herons nest in Munlochy Bay where fulmars are colonising. Between Ethie and South Sutor shags are now breeding on the cliffs.

The Moray Basin is a famous resort of wintering wildfowl. Andrew Currie, of the Nature Conservancy, kindly gives this account of the work of many dedicated local ornithologists. "Wigeon is the most important species. Numbers have sometimes exceeded 25,000, perhaps 5 per cent of the west European population. The entire Iceland wigeon population also possibly passes through on migration. At Nigg Bay over 11,000 have been recorded, although numbers have fallen recently. Mallard, teal and shelduck are all local breeders. About 400 pintail occur during some winters, mainly in Dornoch Firth and Nigg and Longman Bays. Pochard and tufted ducks also winter here, and inland at Loch Eye and other freshwater lochs, and as many as 350 tufted duck sometimes gather in Beauly Firth near the entrance of the Caledonian Canal. Scaup winter near Edderton Bay and, with goldeneye, also congregate at the Invergordon Distillery outflow. In all, over 600 goldeneye regularly winter in the three firths. The Cromarty Firth holds winter flocks of red-breasted merganser, and the Beauly Firth often contains large flocks of up to 800 goosander. These follow the sprat fishery. Both species breed in the area. More than 1,000 eiders may be seen, mainly between Brora and Dornoch, and many breed there. Over 2,000 common scoter are found between Brora and Burghead. And up to 700 velvet scoter and over 500 long-tailed ducks are sometimes counted. On 18th November 1972, 5,912 common scoter and 2,276 long-tailed duck were counted from an aeroplane.

"The flocks of mute and whooper swans are fewer than in the past. Mutes are widely-spread and stay to breed; but whoopers tend to concentrate between Nigg Bay and Dalmore Distillery during winter only. They feed on inland fields although recent disturbance has probably upset their pattern. Greylag geese use Moray Firth from autumn to spring. Up to 1,500 frequent Loch Eye until it freezes and 700 may be seen in Udale and Munlochy Bays and Beauly Firth.

"Few winter, but between late March and May, up to 2,500 pinkfeet sometimes occur in Beauly Firth and up to 3,000 in Nigg Bay and on nearby Nigg Hill. Loch Eye is one of the only two east coast wintering sites of Greenland white-fronts; about sixty are sometimes recorded. Canada geese from known parts of Yorkshire also use Beauly Firth as a moulting area. These birds are then flightless. Now scarce vagrants, brent geese formerly wintered locally in vast numbers.

"Recent developments have disturbed geese and ducks in the Moray Firth, but the Nature Conservancy, Scottish Wildlife Trust, C. G. Headlam and other local naturalists are carefully monitoring these important populations for the Wildfowl Trust and other national bodies."

Many waders winter here. Between Loch Brora and Burghead on 21st January 1973, recorders counted (in round numbers) 7,000 oystercatchers, 500 lapwings, 100 ringed plovers, 2 grey plovers, 125 golden plovers, 200 turnstones, 6 common snipe, 1,600 curlews, 3,250 bar-tailed godwits, 5,000 redshanks, 2 greenshanks, 6,750 knots, 40 purple sandpipers, 4,500 dunlin, 28,000 waders altogether. Wader watchers will thus find plenty of birds to count.

The magnificent bens of Central and Wester Ross have many attractive bird haunts. A few years ago, while my friends sought dotterels and snow buntings on the tops, I worked a little glen where greenshanks had chicks hiding in the rushes. One angry greenshank mobbed a heron and chased a sandpiper and a common gull from a tiny promontory. I later heard two more cock greenshanks joyflying above loch and flows where golden plovers, curlews, snipe and sandpipers had broods. There were red grouse on grass-heaths, wheatears on stones and ring ouzels on boulders. Above a golden eagle floated to its eyrie on a bluff. On a higher ridge one friend had already found a dotterel's nest and broods of ptarmigan.

Farther west is real wild Highland country, with eagles and peregrines, greenshanks and divers. There are grand bird grounds where you could spend a lifetime and always continue to discover. Small colonies of redwings are now well established here; in 1966 there were more than twenty nesting pairs.

There are three fine Nature Reserves in West Ross. In the old pines of the Beinn Eighe Reserve, crossbills sometimes, and siskins regularly, nest. You really must explore this tract of old Caledonian Forest and the islands of Loch Maree. Snow buntings and dotterels have nested on these hills and ptarmigan are on most tops. Golden eagles and peregrines, buzzards and ravens are on the bens, and black-throated divers on the lochs.

Farther west, the Inverpolly Reserve contains many different habitats. Fulmars nest on the coast, shags, great black-backed and lesser black-backs on marine islands. There are also scattered pairs and small communities of greylag geese and eiders. On inland crags you find golden eagles, peregrines, buzzards and ravens. Ravens also nest on coastal cliffs. Greenshanks feed on loch and river, but nest on higher stony flats; snipe bleat and curlews sing over grass-heaths and wet moors. A few pairs of merlins hunt the meadow pipits and wheatears. In the higher hills snow buntings have already been recorded in summer and ptarmigan hold territories.

But perhaps the birchwoods of Inverpolly are its greatest glory. James Fisher found the forest quite a friendly place, "where the sandstone sits on the gneiss and the precipices give

40

way to slopes, birchwoods grow in shelter, particularly by the shores of lochs". Here, in the birches, small groups of wood warblers sing and breed and willow tits have nested in soggy places. At dawn and dusk blackcocks have leks and woodcocks croak over the clearings. Redwings have already settled.

If you love lonely islands, why not take your tents to the Summer Isles and watch the social life of greylag geese? Do peregrines still fight it out with ravens here? Do herons and otters still harry the geese on Eilean A'Chleirich? On these quiet charming islands you will have peace to think and watch.

Yet all is not wild in Wester Ross. Collared doves nest at Aultbea; large groups of lesser redpolls sometimes show near Gairloch; and pied flycatchers have nested at Dundonell and at Torridon. Whitethroats sing in many softer glens.

Ever since the 1860's naturalists have expected great northern divers to nest in the western Highlands or on northern islands. On 23rd June 1970, while fishing among wooded islands on a loch in Wester Ross, Eric Hunter saw a large diver with a black head "in sharp contrast to the grey head and hind neck of the black-throated diver". This strange diver had two young, which often dived and were hard to see against the background of loch and shore scrub. Hunter took no chances. He watched and noted. "The birds were undoubtedly great northern divers." It has taken 100 years before the dream of Saxby and Harvie-Brown has come to pass!

Opposite: The red grouse is a valuable economic asset. These are territorial animals. In autumn dominant cocks win territories and mates. Defeated or less aggressive cocks and mateless hens later form surplus packs which territory-holders continuously chivvy.

Below left: Ben Nevis. This is golden eagle country. There are ptarmigan and wheatears on the ridges and snow buntings are again singing and nesting in the high corries. Pine, birch and alder woods grow in Glen Nevis.

Below right: Cock wheatear with food in bill. Wheatears nest on stony ground from the valley floor to highest corries and ridges.

43

Left: Loch Tulla, Argyll. Crossbills sometimes nest in the old pines and greenshanks court beside the loch. Golden eagles are in nearby glens.

Right: Curlew in a peat hag. This large moorland wader is scarcer in the west than in the east Highlands.

Left: Young herons in the nest. Note the cold yellow eyes and spiky feathers. Herons usually build large nests in the tops of high trees where the young stay for nearly eight weeks.

Centre: Golden plover chicks. These lovely golden balls of fluff sometimes stay twenty-four to thirty-six hours, or even longer, in the nest; longer than any other British wader chicks.

Right: Red-throated diver brooding eggs beside a tarn. Red-throats prefer small lochans to larger lochs. Why not make an ecological comparison between food and habitats of our two Highland divers?

46

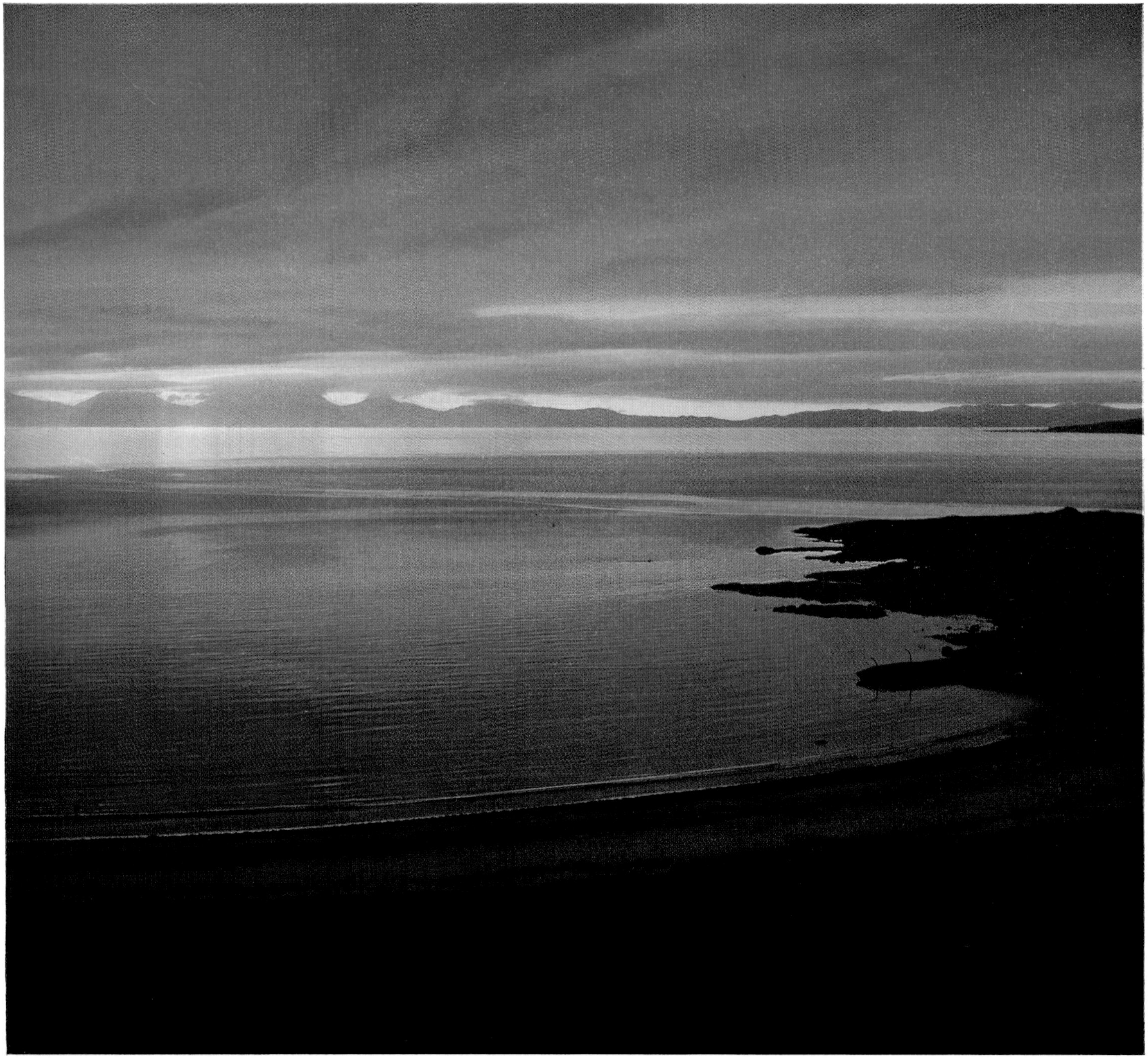

Opposite: The Paps of Jura. There are golden eagles, peregrines and ravens on the cliffs, and hen harriers, short-eared owls and arctic skuas on the moors.

Below left: Great black-backed gull on nest and eggs.

Below right: Lesser black-backed gull brooding.

Note the lesser black-back's greyer mantle. The great black-back's larger size, blacker back, pinkish legs and deeper calls are the field marks. In many parts of the Highlands and Islands great black-backs seem to be thriving at the expense of the smaller species.

Left: Shag and kittiwakes on their nests on sea-cliffs. Shags have exceptionally interesting social and sexual displays and kittiwakes dispose of hatched eggshells differently from any other British gull.

Right: Chough, our rarest crow-bird, feeding young. In March 1974, 91 were counted on Islay and over 20 on the Argyll mainland where a pair has probably nested. Choughs are also now nesting on Colonsay.

West Inverness and Argyll

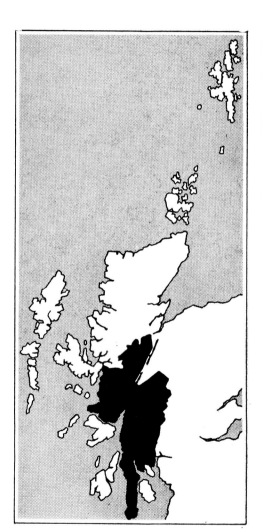

Estate roads and land-rover tracks lead far into this wild country of high hills and deer forests. But birdmen seldom use them. The last of our old Highland ospreys nested here. In 1899 Cherry Kearton stood waist deep in Loch Arkaig to take that remarkable photograph of a hen osprey balancing on a withered stump above the eyrie. For a few years longer the ospreys still maintained—probably until 1908 on Loch Arkaig and possibly 1916 on Loch Loyne. But Scandinavian ospreys are now colonising. You may be lucky enough to find a pair nesting in Lochaber. Just think of it! You watch an osprey fishing in a loch and when it has plunged and caught a fish you follow it into the hills. Then, perhaps, one day you will hear those weak musical scolding cries, and see the two ospreys circling over an old tree. Sit well up the hill and let the hen go back to eggs. See the cock fly in with a fish between his claws. Listen to the interchange of calls as he flaps in and watch the two lovely birds raise their wings before the cock slips on to the eggs and the hen carries the trout to her feeding tree. Come back later and look in wonder as the hen feeds her chicks and the cock brings them fish. I only ask you to keep your secret. But this is only one glorious possibility in grand country where so much is almost certain.

Many golden eagles nest in these steep angular hills; but in the early 1960's few reared young. The dieldrin dressing used in sheep dips was slowly poisoning them; now the voluntary ban on this toxic has apparently succeeded. In Argyll and West Inverness eagles are recovering. Peregrines nest in big cliffs and crags. Why not spend a few days watching a courting pair? There the tiercel gives rusty creaking cries as he scoops hollows on the ledges of that buttress. Look at the two great hawks in their aerobatics and skyplays. What fun they have! The tiercel dives at high speed, the falcon rolls over. They seem as one, then they flash apart. Or see them mock the actions of the food-pass. It all happens so quickly that it quite baffles your eyes. Later, when the falcon has laid up, watch the real food-pass and marvel at its split-second execution. There a small dark speck has dropped from the tiercel's talons and the falcon has rolled over on her back and caught it; now she flaps back to a ledge while the tiercel briefly broods the red-brown eggs on the overhung shelf above. Often you also hear the harsh screams of falcons and the grumbling croaks of ravens in battle over the glen. Time after time the peregrine stoops with half-closed wings and the raven tumbles on its back to present a huge Jewish beak to the falcon as she swishes past, zooms up and stoops again.

Peregrine and golden eagles are not the only special birds of the Lochaber hills. In the past, snow buntings have nested in the huge corries of Ben Nevis. Search them if you can. Snow birds have also bred in hills west of Loch Treig and also probably on spiky bens between Glengarry and Glen Quoich. Why not climb Spidean Mialach and spend a few shivering hours in early morning listening in the corries? Few western hills have the broad backs and long ridges that dotterels love; you should choose those that look like stranded whales. Dotterels have nested. If you do find nest or brood you will have added your little bit of history. Note every bird that you meet with on the tops. Above all, count the ptarmigan. Your notes will greatly help those who are studying their numbers and distribution.

In the lower glens there are fine things to do and see. Glengarry and the flows and hills around are famous greenshank haunts. Fifty years ago Norman Gilroy described his loneliness in these hills. "It was a long dreary trek to those tarns far up Greenfields Burn and beyond Meall an Odhar. In all my life I do not remember having experienced such a feeling of intense isolation and remoteness as I felt on reaching them. Unsheltered, inhospitable, absolutely devoid of life—the sheer pitiless desolation of this place on this utterly abominable morning of May was almost cruel. What a difference the sunshine would have made. What magic would it have wrought!"

New forests and hydro-electric schemes have greatly changed lovely Glengarry, but the hills and flows around Tomdoun are still haunts of our most exciting Highland bird. Wood sandpipers have already nested in Lochaber. Walk far, listen and look hard; you may find them. These marshes belong to moorland birds and the red deer. On these desolate grassy moors there are also golden plovers which few ever watch. Derek Ratcliffe writes: "The biggest blank on my map is the mid-west—from Argyll to north-west Ross and especially West Inverness, where ornithologists never seem to go." You can help to put this right. Where do dunlins nest in these grey flows? Do they form little breeding groups as they do among dubhlochans in Sutherland? How are lapwings and oystercatchers distributed? What is the breeding-density of red grouse? Why not work the barren bumps and flats between Fort William and Mallaig? Black-throated divers nest here and red-throats nearer the coast. In the late 1960's whooper swans also probably nested on at least one western loch. On the streams yellow-breasted cock grey wagtails stand on stones, flirting black white-rimmed tails or they fly dancing through the air. See that cock flutter like a butterfly from rock to bank or back again, or watch him court the hen; with tail erect and bill upturned, he shows off his black gorget. These enchanting little birds are always full of life and movement. Yet no Highland naturalist has really tried to count or understand them. There will also be warm evenings in May with just enough wind to keep away the midges, when you sit beside loch waters and watch sandpipers wickering on the stones or dippers flying over mountain streams.

In the Great Glen and in other parts of Lochaber, and in Sunart in Argyll, there are fine woods and small relicts of former forests where few now watch birds. Our native crossbills now breed here. Groups of siskins nest in the Great Glen, but we know little about their numbers, food and fluctuations. Do crested tits now ever nest here? In 1968 Douglas Weir saw a crestie sitting on a fence post between Loch Arkaig and Glengarry. There are also a few old and shaky records in the literature, but you may be the first to authenticate a nest.

These woods hold the usual groups of pinewood birds. Chaffinches and coal tits dominate mid-wood and willow warblers the fringes. Tiny goldcrests flutter in the canopy and creepers zig-zag up tree trunks; but you hear pied woodpeckers more often than you see them. Discover all that you can about the owls. Do tawnies dominate the edges and are long-ears scarce, as I used to find in Rothiemurchus and Abernethy in the 1930's?

There are also some grand broad-leaved woods. Oak, birch and alder grow on the south-facing slopes of Loch Arkaig. Glen Loy has pines and birches and Glen Nevis has birch and alder by the river. Fine oaks and birches grow north of Loch Hourn and old oaks in Ard-gour; and along the coastal strip are more fragments of the great oak woods of the past. All these woods need careful study. Look out for bramblings or redwings in the birches and for pied flycatchers and willow tits in soggy alders. Do goshawks ever breed in these almost forgotten northern woods? Carefully compare the density and distribution of all woodland birds in pine and broad-leaved woods with those in similar forests in Strathspey. Chaffinches and willow warblers nest in all woods, but great, blue and long-tailed tits favour oak and birch. Here there are more song thrushes than mistle thrushes, blackbirds prefer sunny places close to cottages, and groups of cock redpolls loop above the birches.

Listen for the ecstatic silvery trill of cock wood warblers in the oaks. What delightful little birds! In late spring and early summer wait for that soft mournful little *pew* call. Both cock and hen give these cries but, off nest, the hen uses them more persistently. Follow the cries and try to spot the hen; she will lead you quite a dance as she often feeds far from the nest. Now you see her. She shifts, and moves, and flutters, and calls and calls. At last she leaves the canopy and drops from that oak onto a small stump or sapling. Then up she flies again and still she calls. Soon she flies away again, but do follow that *pew* cry. Now she is back. Like a falling leaf she flutters to that dead upturned branch. There she goes! She flies laterally a few yards and then drops abruptly almost like a stone. She is silent now. Carefully mark where she dropped and gently tap among the brown mast or fallen bracken. Up she flies and flutters and cries again. In the little domed nest, partly below the ground, are five or six small white, boldly-speckled eggs.

Remote Corrour Forest in south-west Inverness holds good habitats for ducks. Mallard, teal, sometimes gadwall, merganser and goosander, all harbour here. Dippers and common sandpipers haunt burn and loch and curlews and snipe the wetter moors and hollows. South-west of Loch Ossian a few greenshanks nest on the flows and dunlins breed near Loch Ghuilbinn. Golden eagle, peregrine and raven nest on mountain cliffs and kestrels on lower crags. Ptarmigan are on the tops and golden plovers on high grasslands. But I have yet to hear of nesting dotterels.

Red-throated divers wail on tarns and black-throats and dabchicks sometimes breed on small ponds close to Corrour Station. Many siskins sometimes nest in pines close to Loch Ossian; and there are also redpolls, chaffinches, and a few bullfinches. In summer redstarts, wood warblers and spotted flycatchers are found here (D. F. Goodfellow). Do redwings and fieldfares now ever stay to nest and are there rare boreal waders on the flows?

Windswept Ardnamurchan, the most westerly point in the British mainland, has golden eagles, peregrines and ravens nesting on its cliffs. Inland is much softer country. Grasshopper warblers have nested and chiffchaffs sometimes sing among the rhododendrons of Acharacle. Wood warblers and redstarts are also there. Strange birds sometimes arrive. In March 1953, Professor M. F. M. Meiklejohn saw four garganey drakes and a duck on the River Shiel and on 6th July 1968, F. C. Best watched an alpine swift flying over sea cliffs between Kilchoan and Ardnamurchan Point!

In the green craggy hills of North Argyll you see golden eagles far more often than in the Cairngorms; but in the 1960's they suffered much from pesticides. In 1965 Lockie and Ratcliffe found only ten nesting pairs in the twenty known territories investigated. But by 1969 these eagles had recovered and were again nesting with normal success. The peregrine story is less happy. These south-west Highland falcons probably winter in districts where they prey on poisoned carrier pigeons. In Lorne and Morvern, Ratcliffe lately found fewer active eyries than he had expected.

South and mid-Argyll have a wide range of habitats—mountain, loch and moor, conifer forest and mixed woods, arable and pasture land, sea cliffs, rocky and shingly shores, and vast sand dunes and mudflats. This is country which I used to hunt for golden eagles. Here I first learnt that the cock eagle brooded eggs. On the first day, huge, black and perfect-winged, the hen flopped off her eyrie. The next time, I watched a much smaller eagle with a missing pinion feather leave the single egg. How I loved my eagle-hunts and how my heart fluttered when I could see the black crags at the end of green and almost endless glens! Once I remember climbing into a huge rocky horseshoe corrie. On the way up I almost touched a sleeping red stag with my stick. How it ran and bounded! A few hundred yards farther on I found the eagle brooding on an eyrie less than ten feet up the cliff; for about ten minutes I gazed at the huge tail projecting from it. How clumsy that eagle looked as it suddenly rose and stood above its eggs, then flapped away just above my head. These Argyll eagles still maintain. In 1970 friends found that ten out of thirteen breeding pairs successfully reared young; they also met with two non-breeding pairs. In 1973 M. J. P. Gregory and A. Gordon found an eyrie from which three eaglets flew.

Hen harriers are now probably the commonest hawks in young conifer plantations in Knapdale and other parts of south and central Argyll; they sometimes breed in loose nesting groups. One winter day, while counting geese between Lochgilphead and Mull of Kintyre,

Seton Gordon was the first naturalist to photograph the magnificent whooper swan at a Scottish nest.

my friends recorded more hen harriers than kestrels or buzzards. Merlins are scarcer, but are found in south and mid-Argyll throughout the year. Here, too, ospreys have been seen a-wing, but no nest has yet reached the published records. There are many ravens, but in Lorne and Knapdale Ratcliffe found them scarce. In 1938, while two friends and I were searching for an eagle's eyrie, a raven slipped off a small crag. Scarcely three weeks before the keeper had shot the hen at a nest here. As the new nest was only ten feet up, my friend scrambled up and looked in. He almost fell! The cock's new mate had laid five erythristic (red) eggs—the first ever found on the Highland mainland. But the speed with which that cock had replaced his mate was not really surprising. In the 1930's ravens and golden eagles in mid-Argyll probably carried a non-breeding surplus. We knew most of the hen eagles by their eggs, but seldom found the same hen in the same territory for more than two consecutive years. Mortality was heavy, but numbers were maintained.

The Argyll hills are full of lochans. In summer black-throated and red-throated divers nest sparingly and common and black-headed gulls have colonies. Greenshanks have nested near Oban, and in Black Mount I have watched them courting beside Loch Tulla. In spring I once watched a pair of whooper swans on a remote tarn. Seton Gordon photographed nesting whoopers in Argyll. Wood sandpipers have arrived. In 1967-69 Ivan and Mary Hills watched these lovely waders singing over a complex of desolate tarns and flows.

The dominant grass-heaths carry fewer red grouse than purer heather country, but in spring and autumn they crow, display, and fight for territories. In open glades, among birches, blackcocks have leks. On my way to eagle glens on early mornings I often stopped to listen to their sharp hissing and soft *rookoos*.

In Knapdale, the cock short-eared owl now carries out his spring flights. You often hear him booing before you pick him up high in the grey west Highland sky. Other birds are also settling. Crossbills are nesting, but we do not yet know whether these are immigrants from the last irruption. But these birds may form breeding groups here as in Dumfries. Carefully compare their calls with any crossbills nesting in the old pines around Loch Tulla. Argyll could help us to understand the complex relationships between native and colonising crossbills. The hoodie/carrion crow line apparently lies across Knapdale; jays are already nesting in these woods, and magpies, though still scarce, are colonising.

On the high tops there are ring ouzels and wheatears in the corries. Snow buntings have been recorded in summer, but no one has found nest or brood. Yet there is plenty of good scree on Ben Cruachan and other hills. There are fewer ptarmigan than in the central and eastern Highlands; but you should find enough to watch. In Cowal, ptarmigan nest down to 2,000 feet or slightly lower.

There are many bird haunts on this long coastline. Choughs still nest on one mainland cliff.

Hugh Blair found black guillemots nesting on Loch Linnhe and on The Creag and Pladda, islands off Lismore. He watched these tysties flying in with fish in beak and found their eggs sucked under a hoodie's nest. On small islands in the Firth of Lorne and Loch Linnhe robins and twites were almost neighbours. Many coastal islets have colonies of great and lesser black-backed and herring gulls; but we know little about their numbers and relationships. Common and arctic terns and black guillemots are dispersed along the coast. In summer and autumn, on both sides of Kintyre, gannets fish and fulmars now nest. Oystercatchers and ringed plovers breed on the shores, redshanks on saltings, and lapwings in the fields. A few dunlins, bar-tailed godwits and greenshanks winter.

The long indented sea coast and the inland lochs have few good wildfowl refuges. In south Argyll, Atkinson-Willes mentions Holy Loch and Loch Eck, Dunoon, Loch Gilp and West Loch Tarbert-Kilberry in Knapdale and Polliwilline Bay, Kintyre, as wintering haunts. Here groups of mallard, teal and particularly wigeon winter. 600 wigeon have been recorded on Loch Gilp, 85 mergansers and 45 goldeneyes on West Loch Tarbert and 50 teal in Polliwilline Bay. A few eider, shelduck and mute swans also use these haunts. The few dedicated observers now covering this huge country have achieved miracles, but they do need your help and enthusiasm. Do give both in good measure.

On the south mainland coast geese are scarce, but about 400 whitefronts have been recorded on wet fields close to Campbeltown airfield. These roost on inland hill lochs. Whitefronts haunt mainland mudflats opposite Gigha; a few greylags and barnacles likewise winter on this coast. There are also scattered flocks of tufted ducks and pochards. Mid-Argyll counters and observers also record a few pintail, shoveller, scaup, long-tailed duck, velvet scoter and smew, whooper swans on passage, and in winter the odd Bewick's swan. The Tayinloan-Isle of Gigha stretch of water is a good watching point for wintering waterfowl and marine birds. Sandy Gordon claimed 50 divers, of all three kinds, in one sweep of his telescope. You can also watch Slavonian grebes at sea, common and velvet scoters, snow buntings, petrels, and other sea birds.

Northwards from the Point of Knap the mainland coast is poor in wildfowl haunts. Fair flocks of mallard, teal and wigeon, and fewer eider, goldeneye, merganser, shelduck and mute swans winter on Loch Sween. Here also are a few whoopers, mainly in November, and 100 or more wintering barnacles and greylags. Farther north small gaggles of whitefronts winter on Lismore.

No one can write about bird-watching in Argyll without realising the immensity of the challenge. Before you meet it, do buy Marion Campbell's *Check List of the Birds of mid-Argyll*. This costs 5p, at the Scottish Centre for Ornithology. Believe me, it is the best bob's worth in Scotland!

An oystercatcher or seapie approaching its three eggs among the stones. Found on many rocky shores in the Inner Isles, oystercatchers have fascinating piping displays, which Julian Huxley was among the first to study.

The Inner Isles

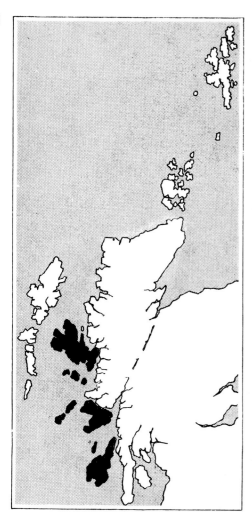

Each lovely Inner Isle is different for birds. For sheer beauty, Skye has almost everything—the spikes and towers of the black and red Cuillin, fine headlands and sea cliffs, long fjords and inviting offshore islands, vast peat moors with tarns and lochs, and some older woods and many new plantations. There are days when the island is hard or misty but others of melting softness and of incredible colours.

To the orthodox bird-watcher Skye is living on its past. Less than 100 years ago no other headlands could compare with these, where Victorian hunters spoke of the sea eagle in familiar terms. "The white-tailed eagle has a very different look to the golden eagle, as its tail is so much shorter and the wings broader and more rounded. When seen from above, the grey head and neck and white tail are very apparent and the yellow feet show at a great distance." In those exciting decades forty of these sea eagles sometimes gathered on carrion and nine or ten pairs had eyries between Loch Brittle and Cop-na-How Head. But by the turn of the century this great bird had almost gone. We must now study the sea eagle's ecology in the context of the nineteenth-century economy in the Highlands and Islands. Did the growth of sheep farming in Skye, for example, produce so much live and dead mutton that these ernes began to carry a non-breeding surplus? Were low status birds the real lamb killers? Did man alone destroy the erne or were there more subtle causes? Surely we can learn from Scandinavian experience. For some years non-breeding flocks of ravens have shown in Skye. Is it mere coincidence that in 1965 the Secretary of State withdrew protection from ravens here? I look forward to some stimulating research.

The sea eagle was not the only loss. By 1904 choughs had almost disappeared and hen harriers were in decline. But Skye still has much to offer. More golden eagles than ever now nest on inland mountains and they have replaced the ernes on some sea cliffs. Peregrines are fewer, but short-eared owls are again nesting in new plantations and their fringes. Hen harriers will return to many former haunts. But why wait? There is no better country for watching ravens. Why not study the relationships, feeding ecology and breeding density of ravens and buzzards in Skye? I have watched a flock of about fifty ravens in the air and would greatly like to know more about its composition. Are there potential or former breeders in these groups? We must learn from every raven shot or destroyed. There is so much to learn about this most intelligent bird. On a Skye cliff I have watched two ravens visiting a nesting pair; the four birds, croaking quietly, circled round one another, but did not fight or challenge. Was this a social call of a related pair? Do coastal ravens have the same food as inland pairs or groups? Do all largely subsist on sheep carrion and is there a significant relationship between lambing and egg-laying dates? We must also discover whether there is real difference between the breeding success of hill and coastal groups.

There are a few greenshanks in the Cuillin foothills in south and central Skye. Until recently these small groups were the most westerly regular breeding greenshanks in the world. Yet no one has systematically studied their behaviour, numbers and breeding success. This could lead to interesting comparative results.

In the high Cuillin record every ptarmigan that you see and remember that snow buntings, already nesting in Wester Ross, may soon extend to Skye. Do note the colour of the rump patch of any cock snow bird seen in summer.

I have never worked the Tokavaig ash and hazel wood in Sleat which grows on Durness limestone. Comparison between this wood and others in the south could be of great interest. Siskin groups are now breeding on Skye as on Rum. In Wester Ross redwings and pied flycatchers are already nesting. Has either now spread to the older birchwoods? Discover all that you can about redstarts and wood warblers here. The coasts of Skye are not rich in large sea-bird colonies, but do compare numbers, distribution and species, with those found on mainland cliffs and on other islands.

South of Skye are the Small Isles of Canna, Rum, Eigg and Muck. On the Nature Reserve of Rum, Nature Conservancy ecologists are managing the herds of red deer and learning much about the natural history of a wonderful island. In all Britain no colonies of manx shearwaters are quite so exciting as those on the high gabbro mountains in south-east Rum. Here on high screes and ridges, upwards of four miles from the sea, shearwaters nest in thousands. Peter Wormell, Bill Bourne and others have already started to discover how a mountain colony ticks. How wonderful to camp among these birds. No one knows how each bird finds its burrow in the dusk. "In the evening they wait offshore in large 'rafts' until about half an hour before midnight; then they rise and fly high into the mountains. As they approach their rocky nesting slopes they fall silent and fly straight towards their burrows, near which they start to scream. Individual calls, merging into a continuous roar for an hour or more." In August 1973 Bruin, Roger Weatherly and Calum Mackenzie spent three nights with the shearwaters here. In the burrows they heard adults grunting roughly and the chicks peeping to them. One call sounded like the twang of an elastic band. By the light of a Tilley lamp they saw a shearwater dragging a wing almost at their feet. It was a great, weird and fantastic experience.

For fifty days, or more, manx shearwaters brood their single eggs; cock and hen alternately sitting or fasting for spells of one to six days. The off-duty bird now sometimes travels hundreds of miles to a distant feeding ground, to restore its strength and brooding urge. At least that is what manx shearwaters do in Wales. But no one knows where Hebridean shearwaters go to fish, or how they time and share their brooding stints.

57

The parents brood the grey downy chick for about a week. From thenceforward they feed it irregularly, sometimes only once in several days. But if both old shearwaters arrive on the same night, the chick "often puts on half its own weight overnight". After about two months the parents themselves are feeding on larger fish, but they visit the chick less often. By now the old birds are moulting, but the chick is as fat and heavy as they are. Then, for the last ten days, the shearwaters abandon the portly nestling, leaving it to starve in the burrow, at the mouth of which it flaps to strengthen its wings. Finally, some time after the seventieth day, a slimmer and stronger chick launches itself against a headwind and makes for the open sea. At least that is how Lockley discovered that shearwaters leave burrows on small islands; but how do mountain chicks reach salt waters so many miles away? Do they really stay longer in the burrow and then glide past waiting predators in the dusk? How do golden eagles catch the shearwaters? Do they hunt them in the gloaming? It makes me wish to go to Rum to learn some answers.

Rum has other sea birds. Fulmars are colonising, but no storm or forked-tailed petrels now nest. Kittiwakes are in good numbers. Great black-backs are dispersed around the coast, but in the 1960's there were fewer lesser black-backs than herring gulls. Guillemots and razorbills nest freely on the southern cliffs.

There are raptors on the island. Sea eagles nested until 1907; they shot the last survivor in 1911 or 1912. Until about 1886 at least five pairs of golden eagles nested on Rum. They then shot and trapped them. But since the early 1950's at least three pairs have annually laid eggs. Have these golden eagles taken the erne's place on sea cliffs? They certainly sometimes feed young herring gulls and manx shearwaters to their young. A pair of peregrines and one or two pairs of merlins also sometimes nest. Sparrowhawks have reared young in Kilmory Glen. There was also a crossbill's skull in a long-eared owl's nest here.

Watch and record all the small birds nesting in the stands of soft and hard wood and in the spinneys. In the 1960's wood warblers probably nested every year. Woodcock also breed in the wetter woods.

Muck, Eigg and Canna pose many problems. Why have storm petrels never firmly settled? Did brown rats and otters alone destroy the large colonies of manx shearwaters on Eigg? Are Atlantic gales really responsible for the lack of guillemots, razorbills and puffins on Eigg's western cliffs? Why do lesser black-backs thrive so well on Muck where great black-backs are fewer? On Eigg and Canna do golden eagles prey on the sea-bird colonies? Can the feeding ecology of these island pairs help to explain why golden eagles have never filled the sea eagle's place on the sea cliffs of the Northern Isles? On what do the ravens feed? Why have they fared much better here than on St Kilda and North Rona?

The croftlands are not rich in birds. But why do corncrakes apparently survive on Canna where former large corn bunting groups are now extinct?

Tiree and Coll, low undulating green islands of Lewisian gneiss, have long sandy beaches and rocky shores, large sand dunes, sea-meadows and worked grasslands, moors, farms and lochs. But Ceann a'Mhara in Tiree is the only high sea cliff. There fulmars are fast increasing and about 600 pairs of kittiwakes nest. Razorbills have completely replaced large groups of guillemots; tysties are few. I do not know whether the red-necked phalaropes are still nesting on Tiree but this was the most southerly breeding station in Britain. On Coll red-throated divers nest and a colony of arctic skuas haunt peatlands. On Tiree, merganser, teal and possibly shoveller are nesting less freely, but goosander and pintail are becoming established as breeding birds. On both islands eider and shelduck are common breeders; snipe, lapwings, and a few dunlin nest on Tiree. Among strange anomalies, lesser black-backed gulls continue to outnumber great black-backs on Coll. Robins do not nest on Tiree but occasionally breed on Coll. A few sedge warblers nest, and dunnocks and pied wagtails are colonising. In the 1950's greenfinches and reed buntings nested on Tiree and some now have firmly settled. House sparrows have replaced tree sparrows, but Morton Boyd (1958) recorded corn buntings and corncrakes as nesting freely on both islands. These trends apparently continue.

Mull is a green and lovely island. In the west, Ben More, a great tertiary basalt hill, dominates. Birders enjoy the challenge of these hills where a few ptarmigan linger. Here are also many ravens and buzzards. Why not compare the breeding density and feeding ecology of these groups with those on Skye? Black-throated and red-throated divers nest on the lochans, but no one has counted them. Many questions remain unanswered. In 1890 arctic terns outnumbered common terns by ten to one. Does this ratio still stand? In the late 1940's great black-backed gulls did not nest, but there were many lesser black-backs. Razorbills then nested commonly on the south and western cliffs and on some islands, but guillemots were scarcer. Is this still true? And will bonxies or arctic skuas colonise moors or headlands close to sea-bird cliffs?

Mull has fine woods and good farms. Wood warblers sing among the oaks, and stonechats haunt the fringes after mild winters. The 1954 census showed that there were at least six heronries, with about twenty occupied nests in the largest. Why not look at these and discover any changes? Curlews are on the moors and woodcocks in the woods. Do many golden plovers still haunt higher moors and grasslands? You must seek them there. Beside birchwoods and close to sea-lochs, blackcocks lek. On farms and crofts, corncrakes rasp, but the corn buntings are almost gone. Why have these corn buntings failed when groups on Coll and Tiree apparently still continue? But all is not for the worse. There are now "at least seven or eight active golden eagles eyries" and some claim a dozen breeding pairs. Some golden eagles now breed on sea cliffs once tenanted by ernes, and an inland pair had its eyrie on an oak tree—a most unusual nest-site in Scotland. A few mute swans nest, herds of whoopers often winter round Loch Buie, and small flocks of barnacles graze on small islands off the west coast.

The Treshnish Islands are great lumps of tertiary basalt. The southernmost, the Dutchman's Cap, is a basalt cone 284 feet high. Here peregrines used to nest on the floor of a cave. On The Harp, separated from Lunga, the middle island, kittiwakes, guillemots, razorbills and fulmars nest. In winter barnacles haunt the Treshnish Islands.

We know little about the birds of Iona. The choughs have gone but there is a rookery near the manse. The island has lost its corn buntings but collared doves are pioneering. In June 1968 a rose-coloured pastor was seen feeding with a flock of starlings.

Jura is a grand challenging quartzite island where eagles and peregrines, ravens and buzzards nest. Here a few choughs still linger. There are greenshanks on the flows, but no one seems to have worked them. In Lowlandmans Bay a few whitefronts winter and gaggles of barnacles haunt small sea islands. In 1973 Patrick saw hen harriers, short-eared owls and arctic skuas on the moors and black-throated divers on a tarn—a great island.

The vegetation on the Torridonian sandstone of Colonsay is much richer and more varied than that of Jura. There are some relict oak and other broad-leaved woods which birdwatchers should investigate. A pair of golden eagles often nest on this beautiful island. In 1970 they brought off one eaglet. The island also has some good wildfowl refuges. In mid-Colonsay some lochs carry small winter flocks of mallard, teal and tufted duck and a few wigeon and pochard. Several hundreds of greylags, a small feral flock of Canadas and a few pinkfeet also winter. Off South Colonsay a few wigeon winter in a shallow sound. Many eider and a few barnacle geese also occur off the Oronsay coast. (Atkinson-Willes.)

Islay is the winter home of about one-sixth of the world population of barnacle geese. Here, in the early 1960's, up to 10,000 barnacle have been recorded in February. About 2,000 roost on sandflats off Loch Indaal. About one-fifth of the world population of Greenland whitefronts sometimes gather on Islay; in February peaks of 1,500 to 3,000 have been recorded. These whitefronts usually maintain smaller flocks than barnacles with which they seldom mix. Greylags also winter in large numbers; in the late 1950's and early 1960's up to 500 were often counted.

There are fine duck grounds on Islay. Up to 1,500 scaup roost and feed on shallow waters off the coast; several hundreds feeding on the barley residue from Bowmore and Bruichladdich Distilleries. In autumn mergansers build up to about 250 before dispersing, but

few winter. Flocks of wigeon and eider, however, sometimes reach quite high numbers.
Inland lochs carry fewer ducks, but mallard, tufted duck, pochard and teal are found.
Lochs Ballygrant and Finlaggan also have a few dabblers. In February 1969 Professor
Meiklejohn spotted the first goosander recorded on Islay and also a Canada goose, of medium
size but not of the usual race, flying with a skein of barnacles.

Groups of up to 250 oystercatchers, 100 bar-tailed godwits and small flocks of dunlin, knot,
ringed plover, snipe and turnstone winter round the head of Loch Indaal. Many curlews
and lapwings also roost on the saltmarshes and sandflats but feed on inland farms. (M. A.
Ogilvie and C. G. Booth.)

Rich in breeding birds, Islay has woods, farms, moors, lochs, mountains and sea-cliffs.
Between 3rd and 17th June 1954 Meiklejohn and J. K. Stanford recorded 112 different
species and proved breeding by 73. Common scoter, arctic and little tern and tree pipit
were first breeding records for Islay. In this year chiffchaffs also almost certainly nested;
and the Port Askaig redstarts, with a nest in a stone wall, were the second Islay breeding
record. That memorable trip produced other exciting discoveries. On 7th June a cock
wood sandpiper sang in display above Loch Airidh Dhaibhaidh—the first record of a wood
sandpiper in the Hebrides. At Portnahaven they also saw a cock red-backed shrike in
first-summer dress—another first for the Inner Hebrides.

In the last few years records multiply. In 1969 hen harriers reared a brood on Islay and
great crested grebes nested on Ardnave Loch. In 1963 collared doves nested at Gruinard
Post Office and now also probably breed at Port Ellen and Bridgend. In June ospreys have
prospected. No one knows what next will nest in Islay. Many vagrants are on the record;
rollers and black-headed buntings are among more recent finds.

But Islay has something even better. Choughs still nest on the cliffs. On mild days in early
spring how I love to watch these lovely birds feeding on the short grass above the cliffs.
See them bend forward on red legs to probe and dig with their curved beaks or watch the
hen shiver her wings to prompt the cock to feed her. There he gently bills her crown and
neck. How marvellously these choughs fly! Bounding buoyantly through the air, diving on
half-closed wings, they fling themselves into crevices of rugged cliffs. Watch the choughs
building, carrying wool or grasses in their beaks. Later see the cock feed the hen on the nest
or call her off. You hear those wild ringing distant *kee-ahs* and see one, two or several choughs
flying low above the sea. One after the other they peel off and bound towards their nests. There
the brooding hen raises head and crown feathers and shivers her wings before he feeds her.
Then, off he flies away again. This is a bird which is losing out in Britain and Central Europe.
In 1966 only eleven pairs bred in Scotland, all in Argyll, mostly on Islay and Jura. The hard
winter of 1963 has not helped. Do then let us enjoy our lovely choughs while we may.

The Outer Isles

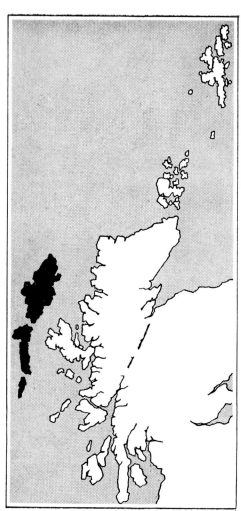

The remote Outer Isles always called Booth and the Old Naturalists. Here were huge cliffs alive with noisy sea-birds and pools and lochans where dainty phalaropes twirled around or flew like swallows across the marsh. Motor cars and the rocket range have now opened up many of these evocative places, but they are still among the most compelling of all British bird grounds.

On the fine sea-bird cliffs of Berneray and Mingulay fulmars, guillemots and razorbills nest in thousands and kittiwakes at least in hundreds. Barra has miles of rocky coast, white sand and machair, and countless tarns. No one has done justice to these birds. Sea ducks and barnacle geese winter beside the Sound and small flocks of wigeon, tufted duck and whoopers haunt Loch St Clair. Across the Sound of Barra, a viaduct links South Uist with the wetlands of Benbecula and thence the north causeway joins Benbecula to North Uist.

In South Uist are high moors and wild hills in the east. Here are golden eagles, ravens and hen harriers. But the island is more famous for its waterfowl and wetlands. The Loch Druidibeg Nature Reserve contains a good sample of native greylag geese. On small islands, where the birch scrub is green in summer, the greylags nest and later take their goslings to richer pasture beside machair lochs. In 1972 sixty-eight pairs nested. What a wonderful haunt for geese!

There are other splendid wildfowl lochs and refuges. Loch Bee holds herds of several hundred mute swans and almost as many whoopers in winter. Fewer barnacles and white-fronts now stay on western machairs, but flocks of over 200 are still sometimes seen. In winter many mallard, teal, wigeon and tufted duck, but fewer pintail and shoveller, scaup and goldeneye harbour here. Tidal waters also carry eider, merganser and shelduck, but fewer scoter and long-tailed duck than the great flocks in the northern isles.

But, to me, the inland lochs, tarns, marshes and machair will always be the challenge. Who knows what you might find? Scaup, whooper swan and spotted crake are always possible.

Flat Benbecula, with its maze of lochs and creeks, has always been in my dreams. With loving care the old hunter unwrapped the cotton wool. "Red-necked phalaropes from Benbecula", he murmured, and told me how he had found the nests on a wonderful misty island! In 1947 a friend found a whooper swan on a nest and eggs, only realising what it was when the hen flapped away. A few greylags still nest and whitefronts winter in bogs around Nunton Moor. Mallard and wigeon dabble on the east coast and greylags and barnacles are around Loch Uskavagh and between the Sound and the North Fords.

At Balranald in North Uist the R.S.P.B. has a Reserve of 1,500 acres of marsh and loch, beach and dune, machair and croftland. Things have changed for the better since 1899 when Richard Kearton hoped to photograph phalaropes in the Western Isles. "Directly I had approached where I had found the bird breeding, I was besieged by a number of boys and girls who asked me whether I wanted to buy phalaropes' eggs. One of the latter told me she

had once sold a clutch for 1/10 and the odd 2d. off the round sum plainly indicated to me the
business acumen of the pedlar". I only wish that phalaropes were now nesting in peace and
plenty. In the early 1870's at least fifty pairs bred in the Outer Isles and even in the 1920's
and 1930's half-a-dozen pairs often nested at Balranald. But for the last few years I read that
not a single chick has been raised on these marshes. I also learn with sorrow that in 1969
there are probably less than six pairs in all the Outer Hebrides. The declining populations
of these lovely phalaropes urgently demands research. In decades when the ranges of many
boreal birds are expanding what has caused that of the phalarope to contract? The Outer Isles
are not the only region where red-necks are in retreat. In 1905 about fifty pairs nested in the
sea-marshes near Belmullet in Co. Mayo; but by 1965 this grand colony had dropped to just
five pairs. Do let us try to discover the causes and confer with ecologists in Northern Europe.
Balranald has other riches. Dunlins rise and fall as if on silvery threads; mallard, teal,
wigeon, shoveller, tufted duck and gadwall nest. In 1969 the rare scaup also bred. Dab-
chick, coot, moorhen, mute swan, water rail, snipe, redshank, twite, skylark and sedge
warbler are all in these splendid marshes; and corn buntings, lapwings and corncrakes nest
on the croftlands. On sand dunes and beaches are eider, red-breasted merganser and shelduck, ringed plover and oystercatcher, and common, arctic and little terns. Rock pipits
dominate the coast, meadow pipits the inland moors. With such a study area at your
disposal why travel further?

Ian Newton noticed many contrasts in the Uists—the barren acid moors and peat bogs in the
east and the rich machairs in the west. Waders love the machair. Lapwings, oystercatchers
and snipe are almost everywhere; redshank, dunlin and sandpipers favour wet loch edges;
ringed plovers nest on sandy or newly-ploughed ground. The phalaropes have a few special
tarns, but more golden plovers nest on the wet flows and moors of Lewis. A few greenshanks
breed in North Uist with Loch an Sticir as their feeding loch and centre. Corncrakes still
rasp around the machair lochs where there are many coots but fewer moorhens. Arctic skuas
are on many flows and moors in North Uist but apparently not in South Uist and Benbecula.
Common and arctic terns have large colonies, but there are only three small groups of
graceful little terns.

The pine and rhododendron plantations beside Loch Druidibeg harbour the only greenfinches and goldcrests on the Uists and the only known pair of long-eared owls. Here is a
large crow roost, a heronry in rhododendrons, and an osprey appeared two years running.
The Hebridean races of song thrush, robin and stonechat are rather scarce, the local race of
wren more plentiful. Blackbirds nest in gardens.

South of the Sound of Harris are fourteen to fifteen pairs of golden eagles and five to six pairs
of peregrines, mostly on east coast headlands. Hen harriers and buzzards are widespread, but
there are few kestrels and merlins. Short-eared owls hunt machair marshes like Balranald.

64

On north-west machairs and on some offshore islands, barnacle geese have grazing grounds; the Monach Islands carry several hundreds. In 1955 they peaked at over 2,000 before flying north. Many Greenland whitefronts also pass by but few overwinter.

North Harris is a complex of smallish granite hills—a good golden eagle and raven country. In these hills where their natural prey is scarce, Jim Lockie reckoned that there was a breeding pair of eagles to roughly every 17,000 acres. No one who carefully works the coast and stony flows of Harris can fail to make ornithological history.

Sometime between 1822 and 1834 Professor William MacGillivray found a greenshank's nest on Harris, the first ever recorded in the Outer Isles. But when writing *The Greenshank* in 1951 I could discover no recent record. However, on 14th June 1973, I. and M. Hills saw a greenshank with two half-grown chicks on a sea meadow in south-west Harris.

Lewis is now less popular with bird-watchers than the Uists and Benbecula. But Harvie-Brown and others knew the island's birds. Because Lewis is almost treeless, the Stornoway woods are of great interest but, to me, resident birds are more important than the strays. How, why, and when did these birds colonise? Have they formed closed communities and how do territory-holders react to prospecting strangers? Colour-ringing might greatly help us. The colonisation by rooks is well documented. In October 1893 a great flock was blown west to Lewis; hundreds were found floating dead round the shore. In the next spring about 200 stayed but did not breed, but in 1895 some nested. Now Stornoway woods hold an immense rookery with hundreds of nests.

In the 1960's other colonists arrived. Creepers first nested in 1962, blue tits in 1963, coal tits in 1965, and great tits in 1966. Many blue tits are now nesting; and coal and great tits are becoming established. Blackbirds, song thrushes, and a few mistle thrushes, now nest regularly; goldcrests, greenfinches and chaffinches are consolidating. Will fieldfares and redwings follow?

Summer migrants are easier to understand. Willow warblers nest in good numbers; chiff-chaffs, whitethroats, spotted flycatchers and sedge warblers have already bred; and collared doves have arrived. What a lot these woods can tell us if we only ask the right questions. W. A. J. Cunningham has made a wonderful start and earned our thanks.

Apart from the Stornoway woods, Lewis is wild and bare. Bonxies and arctic skuas now nest on moors and flows and red-throated divers on peatland lochans. You often hear the divers cackling as they fly from sea to tarn. There are also many dunlin groups.

The coast of Lewis holds many sea-bird colonies. Groups of fulmars and clumps of kitti-wakes and quite a lot of black guillemots nest on the Butt of Lewis. Loch Stiapavat and the machair south of the Butt provide winter haunts for mallard, teal, wigeon, small herds of whooper swans; and flocks of pinkfeet and greylags touch down in spring. Uig has golden

66

Left: The dainty red-necked phalarope has a reversed courtship and sexual differences. We must discover why so few now breed in the Outer Isles where fifty pairs nested 100 years ago. They have much declined in North and South Uist and have disappeared from Lewis and Harris.

Centre: Loch Druidibeg Nature Reserve contains a good sample of our native greylag geese. The greylags nest on small green islands and later take the goslings to richer machair lochs.

Right: Greylag goose brooding. This is a most intelligent social animal. In 1972 sixty-eight pairs nested in Loch Druidibeg Nature Reserve. Ian Newton tells me that '109-124 pairs nested on the whole Hebrides in 1968.'

Left: Gannet landing. The largest gannetry in the world is on Boreray and Stacs an Armin and Lee, St Kilda, where there are now over 59,000 nesting pairs.

Right: Butt of Lewis. Groups of fulmars, clumps of kittiwakes, and quite a lot of black guillemots nest here. This is a fine spot for watching passing gannets.

Left: The unique St Kilda wren. These wrens have whiter eyestripes, are slightly larger, and have paler underparts and warmer brown upperparts than mainland wrens. A few pairs nest in village cleits but most on huge sea cliffs.

Centre: The charming storm petrel at the entrance to its nesting burrow. There are large colonies on St Kilda where all four British petrels nest in high numbers.

Right: The graceful flight of the dynamic fulmar. In this century fulmars have dramatically increased and spread all round the coasts of Britain. In early 1960's nearly 20,000 pairs nested on Hirta, St Kilda.

Opposite: The cock merlin, here brooding, takes a small share in incubation. The merlin, the typical small falcon of the Orkney, Shetland and mainland Highland moors, has suffered from DDT toxics, but is slowly recovering.

Below left: Cock golden plover on nest and eggs. Golden plovers still sing and display high over Orkney moors, but agricultural changes have destroyed many good nesting habitats.

Below centre: Dunlin in the wetlands. In the evening you will hear the dunlin's pea-whistle song and see its yo-yo flights above the bog.

Below right: The Dale, Orkney, with the small hills, valleys and rolling moorland beloved by hen harrier, merlin and short-eared owl. Hobbister and Birsay Moor are other R.S.P.B. moorland reserves in Orkney.

Female hen harrier incubating. In Orkney some cocks have several hens, but these harems do not produce more flying young than monogamous pairs. Hen harriers are now nesting on many mainland moors and in young plantations. They may have spread from Orkney or have colonised from Fenno-Scandia.

eagles in the hills and black-throated divers on some lochs. A few greenshanks now nest on remoter flows. I should like to trace the history of this recent recolonisation. Peregrine, raven and buzzard have eyries on the cliffs. But the sea eagles which Booth hunted on the Park of Lewis have gone. Perhaps snowy owls will take their place on the desolate moors.

Adventurous naturalists have always loved the lonely island outposts. St Kilda and North Rona, the Flannans and Sula Sgeir, all have their champions. The St Kilda group—Dun, Hirta (the largest), Soay and (four miles north-east) Boreray and the great rock pillars of Stac Lee and Stac an Armin are all part of a famous saga. Martin Martin's *A Late Voyage to St Kilda* (1698) set the stage. The Kearton brothers, who photographed the sea-birds and for several weeks lived on St Kilda, first fired my imagination for these romantic islands. I still believe that *Nature With A Camera* is the best and most vivid general account of St Kilda ever written. What hard, primitive, lonely lives these hardy islanders lived. In summer bearded cragsmen performed feats of skill, rockcraft, and courage which would have earned them immortal fame in the Alps or on the Dolomites. In one short sentence, Ken Williamson describes the harshness of human life on St Kilda. "Fulmars, puffins, gannets, guillemots, razorbills and gulls, roughly in that order of merit, provided their food supply and their staple trade in feathers and oil with the world outside." For hundreds of years the St Kildans survived storm and famine on their lonely islands, until in 1930, they were finally forced to quit. Thenceforward, the sea-birds were in command; but a few naturalists still braved the stormy seas. Then, in April 1957, the army posted a small garrison to man a radar station on Hirta. As a bonus, St Kilda and North Rona became Nature Reserves, manned by scientists from the Nature Conservancy.

On St Kilda all four British petrels—fulmar, storm, fork-tailed and manx shearwater—breed in great numbers. The fork-tailed petrel, still one of the least-studied British birds, requires new research techniques. Do mateless males alone perform those fluttering displays at night? Do these strange birds court by sound and do the birds inside the burrows call down those flying and circling in the dusk? How do fork-tailed petrels mate, court, and display inside their burrows? What are the functions of their different calls and cries?

Since 1698 fulmars have nested on St Kilda. In 1961 Sandy Anderson reckoned that about 20,000 breeding pairs were on the Hirta cliffs. Elsewhere, Aberdeen ecologists have discovered much about the fulmar's life. From November onwards, these petrels prospect their future nesting cliffs and by late April are paired and settled on their ledges. Then, for about a fortnight, both birds quit their breeding grounds. Afterwards the cock usually returns a few days before the hen, which soon scoops a hollow on a ledge and there lays her egg. Do fulmars leave the cliffs to prepare and fatten themselves for their eight weeks of brooding? Do they require special food from special feeding grounds? Does their weight change between departure and return? There is certainly much to learn about this unexpected behaviour. The hen now broods the egg for only a few hours while the cock waits on a nearby ledge. But in his first spell of brooding he sits for a whole week or sometimes longer. Thereafter, cock and hen change over at intervals of two-and-a-half to five days. But in the last few days of incubation both birds alternately sit for two days or less and the off-duty partner often waits on the cliff nearby. What factors control these unusual brooding rhythms? Both fulmars brood the squab, often feeding it daily for a further seven or eight weeks. The young fulmar then waits until a gale, roaring against the cliff, helps to give it lift. The largest gannetry in the world is on Boreray and Stacs an Armin and Lee. By analysis of aerial photographs, John M. Boyd estimated that over 44,000 pairs were nesting and that about 14,000 pairs of guillemots were dispersed in 112 colonies; about 18,000 pairs of kittiwakes were also clumped close to the guillemots. Many hundreds of razorbills nest below rocks and boulders or in cracks and crevices. There are a few tysties but puffins breed in tens of thousands.

Research on the predators of St Kilda would be a project of great value. Why do peregrines no longer nest regularly and why are there so few breeding ravens? The St Kildans certainly hated any competitors and savagely suppressed great black-backs and lesser black-backed gulls. Now, fifty to one hundred pairs of great black-backs breed on the St Kilda group and about 100 pairs of lesser black-backs nest on Gleann Mor. Why have lesser black-backs done so well?

There are also exciting wader problems. Many snipe, apparently of Faroe race, nest on old crofts and dry hillsides. When and how did snipe colonise St Kilda? The islanders would have been sore on them. Are these snipe a closed group? What is their breeding rate and recruitment and how do they survive when so many predators are after them? Golden plovers, seemingly of the black-faced race, and stray pairs of whimbrels, have also bred on St Kilda. There are many oystercatchers. Why not compare their habitats, breeding-density, territorial behaviour and nesting success with groups already studied on the Scottish mainland and in Wales?

The unique St Kilda wren is a hardy little bird. In 1904 the Westminster Government passed a Special Act for its conservation. But this was really quite off beam. The hard-pressed islanders—with no such Act to safeguard them—did rob and kill a few wrens in the village cleits but, like wrens in Greenland, almost all these little birds lived on enormous sea cliffs where they were immune from gun and blowpipe. In 1957 Ken Williamson plotted 117 cocks singing on the Hirta cliffs; in good years probably about 200 to 250 pairs breed on the St Kilda group. These wrens have special ecological and territorial adaptations. Work on the Hebridean and northern island wrens offers exciting prospects.

North Rona, about forty miles north-east of Lewis, has no history of recent human struggle.

But leisured, well-heeled Victorians and Edwardians ventured there in small boats with scratch crews. In June 1882, guided by "the strong musty odour which pervaded the inhabited burrows", J. Swinburne dug out twenty-three fork-tailed petrels' eggs. Two years later Harvie-Brown bitterly regretted that he had not brought a crowbar! He took nine eggs— "one broken by Angus's foot"—and seven hens, three of which he graciously released. In later years other pirates briefly landed, but no one seriously studied the petrels until 1936 when John Ainslie and Robert Atkinson camped from 16th July to 12th August. They graphically describe the night-life of the fork-tailed petrels. "The first birds began to arrive soon after dark—a shadowy rushing of wings. They fly in silence. When a company has gathered, the staccato calling begins and soon works up to a pitch. The cries are loud and outlandish; the flight is headlong, at breakneck speed in the darkness. There are collisions— birds tumble to the ground . . . The impression of the night flying is of undoubted excitement and urgency, energy unleashed. It goes on without flagging all night until with the first sight of dawn, the activity gradually dies down."

North Rona has colonies of storm as well as fork-tailed petrels. Fulmars and kittiwakes nest in thousands, puffins in higher numbers. Dominating the sea-bird colonies, great blackbacks prey heavily on puffins and young kittiwakes. In the last decade bonxies have bred; in 1970 there were two pairs, but only one hen laid eggs. Whimbrels may sometimes nest. On 17th July 1949, Ian Pennie watched a pair which "very obviously had young", but he could not spare the time to search.

Seventeen miles west-north-west of Gallan Head are the Flannans and their skerries. Here many fork-tailed petrels nest in broken ground, some quite close to the lighthouse.

Rocky Sula Sgeir, some twelve miles west-south-west of North Rona, holds a famous gannetry. Here, probably since the twelfth century, the Men of Ness have gone by boat to crop the fully-fledged young gannets, known as gugas. The late Jim McGeoch, a hardy Scottish bird-watcher, joined the Men on three guga hunts. "The gugas are snared by long bamboo catching poles, to which is fixed a spring device to seize the bird by the throat, while another member of the crew despatches it. The catch is passed to the top of the cliff by hand from man to man, or by rope. It is then divided equally and each crew carry their own birds to the plucking bothy or small stone fank, where the birds are plucked and singed over strong peat fires. Thereafter, they are split open, the inside and remaining outer skin removed, and are salted and packed into a large beehive-shaped pile ready to await the arrival of the boat". Ashore, after three weeks or more in primitive bothies, the Men re-salt the gugas and sell them in winter. These sales help to pay the cost of the expeditions and give wages to the raiders.

We all have different ideas of fun, sport and conservation!

Orkney

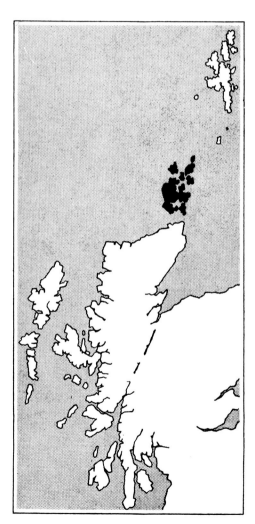

It was May 1932. I had already found my first crested tit's nest in Abernethy Forest and had seen a greenshank jump off eggs on a Sutherland flow. Now I was northward bound; my dream was coming true. Across the Pentland Firth was the hard grey coast of Orkney—and hen harriers, merlins and short-eared owls! A few hours later a friend was driving me over squat hills, through small farms, and past lochs and tarns. As we rounded a bend a blue cock harrier swept across the moor and almost hung above the car. I could hardly wait! At his farm at Howe I found John Douglas in the byre. In rough tweeds, with cap worn backwards, he warmly greeted me. Two bright eyes twinkled in the brownest face that I had ever seen. For the next fortnight this hardy birdman took me in hand. Every morning, at 3 o'clock, I cycled out to meet him. By 8 o'clock Douglas was striding home. On my first day out he showed me golden plovers nesting on mossy ground almost beside his farm; there were four nests in about ten acres. Never since have I seen goldies' nests so close together. At that time Douglas had probably forgotten more about hen harriers than any British bird-watcher had ever known. I never learnt so much in so short a time. On early mornings corn buntings jingled on almost every croft and corncrakes rasped in the fields; and in the evening dunlins purred over bogs. Douglas taught me how to watch hen harriers. I saw the thrilling diving sky-play of one cock and watched another stoop at his brown hen which rolled and slipped away as he almost touched her with his wing. The food-pass of the harriers was most spectacular. The cock flew in with a dark bundle between his claws and a large brown-winged bird flew up to meet him. The two harriers almost came together. The cock dropped what he was carrying, the hen banked, caught it, and in a flash was gliding down. That time I failed to watch her back to eggs. But I later flushed her from a nest in a yellow rushy bottom. I can still hear her weak angry chatter as she rushed at my head.

John Douglas told me that a few cock harriers were bigamous; one fed two different hens near nests in the same long valley. Eddie Balfour, the Orkney birdman, finds that this is now a common practice; but it happened less often in the early 1930's. Some cocks now possess harems of several hens, but these do not produce more flying young than normal pairs. Another mated cock was probably an immature bird as brown as any hen. I spent many hours watching him and her at their nest and eggs. I also saw harriers mating. A grey gull-like cock pursued the hen which pitched on a tuft of long heather on which she flapped her wings. The cock glided and hovered over her; then he also settled and beat his wings. A minute later, with a few quick strong flaps, he had landed on her back.

Eddie Balfour reports that these fine harriers are still doing well in Orkney; there are about fifty pairs on Mainland, Hoy and Rousay. In a bumper year nine pairs nested in about one square mile of moorland.

Why not bury yourself under heather and sit over a nest throughout one long day? Watch the perfect timing of the food-pass and discover exactly how the pair behaves or, like Eddie

You can sometimes find the nest of a short-eared owl by searching the marsh over which the cock is scolding. In many parts of the Highlands short-eared owls now nest in young conifer plantations. Watch the cock arrive with a vole for the sitting hen.

Balfour, study the feeding rôles of cock and hen and what each brings to the growing chicks. Merlins are now probably scarcer than in the 1930's, but about twenty pairs still nest on Mainland and other parts of Orkney where they share hills and valleys with short-eared owls and harriers. Watch both merlins, whinnying angrily, mob the cock harrier whose hen is sitting in the moss. Or see the jack in full gallop over the heather. Few gamer birds fly than these little merlins.

John Douglas insisted that a short-eared owl's nest was usually harder to find than those of hen harrier and merlin; and we certainly worked hard for the three nests that we found. At the first, with a brood of chicks, the hen owl performed fantastic distraction displays on the heather. Our other two nests held full clutches of round creamy white eggs. Now, for the first time, I also watched a cock short-ear dropping, clapping his wings, and booing high above the hill; he was possibly an unmated bird. Short-eared owls have their good and bad breeding years: vole numbers probably determine their breeding density. In 1968 they did particularly well in Orkney, which is a perfect place to study their behaviour, fluctuations and relationships with hen harriers. Orkney needs a field station and long-term research programme. Eddie Balfour's fine work must be continued and expanded.

Since 1945 some kestrels have nested on the ground. These pairs are sometimes dispersed one mile or more apart, but in 1954 Balfour found five nests in one square mile of moor. Most ground-nesting pairs choose nest-sites which are equally suitable for merlins; others lay in overgrown cracks, under heathery banks, or in rabbit holes. Shelducks sometimes compete with them for nest-sites. Heather-nesting wood pigeons, mallards, merlins, short-eared owls and hen harriers are also often close neighbours. In Orkney natural selection is evidently working fast; but no one has studied the origin of this adaptation. The sea-cliffs appear to hold as many pairs as ever, but we know nothing about a possible surplus. Do these heather-nesting kestrels belong to small self-perpetuating pioneer groups which have exploited a new niche? Colour-banding and food analysis could surely lead to much stimulating research.

Orkney has many other problems. Agricultural changes have destroyed many good golden plover and dunlin nesting habitats. The moss where John Douglas showed me the goldies' nests is long since ploughed up. But has anyone tried to compare the breeding density of golden plovers nesting close to coastal farm strips with that of pairs nesting on remoter Orkney moors and in the central and eastern Highlands? Why not also compare the density and territorial behaviour of dunlins in various habitats in Orkney with those on similar ground in the Outer Hebrides?

In dips and valleys many curlews now trill and bubble on quivering wings. Harriers often capture their unfledged chicks. In the 1930's I met with no oystercatchers nesting on inland

79

hills, but some now breed on bare burnt braes. On lower coastal farms do oystercatchers share habitats with lapwings? The richer Orkney farms used to carry the densest breeding groups of lapwings in Britain. A square mile of farmland was sometimes said to hold up to 200 breeding pairs, but the hard winters of 1941-42 and 1962-63 dramatically reduced them. Red-necked phalaropes have apparently ceased to nest on North Ronaldsay, but one or two pairs still sometimes grace the tarns and lochans of another island. In the 1880's a few whimbrels nested on Hoy and Sanday and there was a brood on Hoy in 1889. Now the whimbrels are back again. In 1968 two pairs probably bred on Eday. In these decades we can expect more breeding whimbrels. In 1956 black-tailed godwits reared a brood on Sanday, but they have apparently never become established. Were these godwits Iceland birds? Greenshanks nested on Hoy in 1951, but I understand that this did not lead to further breeding.

The coast, sea cliffs and small islands are a delight to all who love sea-birds. If you are natural pirates go in small boats to the romantic stacks which stand above the hazy or stormy sea. In the 1930's few bonxies bred on Hoy, but by 1961 their numbers had risen to about sixty pairs. These powerful skuas now have colonies on four other islands. Arctic skuas, restricted to Hoy in the 1930's, have also thrived. Hoy now boasts about 150 pairs; and there are breeding groups on Mainland and on several islands. Great black-backed gulls have large 'cities' on Hoy, Calf of Eday, Stronsay and other places. About 4,000 pairs nest on Hoy where there are two wonderful colonies. At Burn of Forse 1,000 to 2,000 pairs have nested and at Stowdale there is another colony of about 700 to 800 nesting pairs (Balfour). There are also two large moorland groups on Mainland, one of which is three miles from the coast. They have replaced lesser black-backs in many haunts. Why not compare the social behaviour in great black-back 'cities' with those in the lesser black-back and herring gull groups which Tinbergen investigated on Walney Island? I have never studied a social animal but I can sense the excitements of discovery. There are fewer lesser black-backs but thousands of herring gulls on sea-cliffs and low islands. These silvery gulls now have large colonies on inland moors. Graceful kittiwakes and sharp-billed guillemots breed together on the big cliffs of Marwick Head, Noup Head, Westray, Calf of Eday, Copinsay, and other crags. Copinsay, the James Fisher Memorial Reserve, is now owned and managed by the R.S.P.B. 10,000 pairs of kittiwakes and 10,000 pairs of guillemots and lower numbers of razorbills, tytsies and puffins nest here.

Far out in the Atlantic hundreds of arctic terns nest on small islands and rocky skerries. The scarcer common terns are in mixed colonies. In 1967 there were four groups of terns on Sule Skerry, about 400 pairs in all, "mostly arctic with the odd common". Lovely sandwich terns also nest here; but numbers fluctuate and colonies shift from place to place. In 1968 about 150 pairs bred on Burray, 80 pairs on North Ronaldsay, and others on Sanday.

Adventurous bird-watchers visited lonely Stack Skerry and Sule Skerry in 1967. On Sule Skerry they reckoned that about 60,000 pairs of puffins were nesting. "As the sun slowly set there seemed to be a continuous stream dropping down into their burrows, each bird carrying a mouthful of small fish". Large colonies of storm petrels were also probably nesting on this stack; and the watchers caught and ringed a fork-tailed petrel there. On Stack Skerry were about 3,500 pairs of gannets, roughly as many non-breeding birds, about 200 pairs of guillemots, and 100 nesting pairs of kittiwakes, "with 400 non-breeding birds present".

Storm petrels nest in great numbers on Auskerry and in smaller numbers on other islands. Few manx shearwaters now breed but fulmars are legion. Since 1950 Aberdeen University researchers have colour-banded fulmars on Eynhallow. George Dunnet tells me that two or three of the fulmars marked in 1950 are still alive. These fulmars start to breed in their tenth year and then have a further eighteen years as adults. Their average life span is twenty-eight years, but some live to the ripe old age of forty to fifty. What exciting discoveries they have made.

Eddie Balfour and Sandy Anderson have studied the distribution and dispersal of cormorants in Orkney, where about 600 pairs nest, two-thirds on the twin islets of Boray Holm and Taing Skerry, and on the Calf of Eday—each with about 200 pairs.

Herons nest on sea cliffs but are not thriving. In 1969 only two pairs nested on Lyra Geo, Yesnaby. In some parts of Britain herons have taken to spearing their own eggs and pitching them out. Toxics probably cause this behaviour. Why not weigh and compare some blown eggshells from Orkney with those from mainland heronries in the pre-toxic period?

Raptors are scarce on mainland and island cliffs. Sea eagles nested on Hoy until about 1865. Once about a dozen pairs of ernes nested on the sea cliffs and a golden eagle inland. The golden eagle is now back to Hoy but it has not filled the erne's niche. Since 1961 buzzards have also settled on Hoy, but by 1970 there were only two nests. Peregrines are doing badly. In 1968 they bred poorly, and in 1969 less than half of the dozen pairs brought off young. Pesticides are probably the cause. Ravens are well dispersed along the coasts, but are not so abundant as in Shetland. Hooded crows are also scarcer.

Quails nest occasionally. Corncrakes are in decline; and corn buntings restricted to a few northern isles. These slumps conform to national trends which we do not yet fully understand.

Orkney is rich in birds of marsh and flow. Red-throated divers nest on tarns and a few dabchicks are still found on Mainland and some northern islands. Up to thirty pairs of mute swans bred on the Lochs of Harray and Stenness where there are large non-breeding groups. A few mutes also haunt brackish inlets, small lochs and tarns on Mainland, and on some larger islands. Moorhens *quek* on weedy ponds, but coots are scarce. Always rare, the secretive water rail has possibly ceased to nest. Snipe drum, dunlins purr, and redshanks yodel in squashy places; but common sandpipers are still decreasing everywhere. Noisy communities of black-headed gulls shift from marsh to marsh and common gulls are in small well-dispersed groups. Teal and mallard are common and increasing and beautiful pintails nest in scattered pairs. Shovellers and pochards have outposts on northern isles and a few wigeon nest on Mainland and elsewhere. Tufted ducks are scarce but are well scattered. As a young man, John Douglas found a long-tailed duck's nest in Orkney. The scarce scaup sometimes breeds; between 1954 and 1959 two pairs nested on Papa Westray and in 1965 one pair bred in North Ronaldsay. Then, in 1969, scaup also nested on west Mainland.

Small stocks of heath and woodland birds nest in Orkney. Lovely cock reed buntings jingle on marshy edges and mild winters help stonechats to survive on Mainland and Hoy. Yellowhammers have decreased; starlings and house sparrows haunt farms and homesteads. Linnets nest freely in gorse and scrubby woods and sometimes in old quarries and on drystone walls. A few tree sparrows have settled in an Eday firwood. Skylarks sing above the richer grasslands, but are not on the high moors where meadow pipits are dominant. Twites still maintain small but well-dispersed nesting groups; a few nest in fuchsia bushes in North Ronaldsay. White wagtails have nested, but pied wagtails are scarce or missing. There are no swifts, swallows are scarce, and house martins are no longer regular nesting birds.

In scrub and garden robins and hedge sparrows hold territories. Orkney cuckoos sometimes lay their eggs in these dunnocks' nests. There are usually many wrens; but hard winters decimate them. A handful of spotted flycatcher and a few willow warblers nest regularly in the softer places. In 1949 blackcaps bred on Shapinsay and in 1965 garden warblers at Binscarth. Collared doves are spreading and many wood pigeons nest in plantations as well as in heather. Goldcrests seldom nest.

Mistle thrushes are extremely scarce but song thrushes and blackbirds plentiful in woods and gardens. Now that sparrowhawks no longer haunt Orkney woods, the few long-eared owls are the only woodland bird-predators.

In 1967 fieldfares nested in a little west Mainland glen. On 1st August both parents were still feeding hungry chicks. Then, in 1969, a second pair reared young in a nest in heather. Redwings have not yet bred in Orkney, but we may soon expect them.

In 1971 I returned to Orkney where I saw great changes. Many of the heathery hills which John Douglas and I hunted for harriers and merlins are now green and reseeded. Marshes are dry and mosses cultivated. But Eddie Balfour continues his stimulating research on the harriers. He now assesses the age of female harriers by the colouring of their eyes. So do go to Orkney. You will love these islands and their exciting birds just as much as I do.

82

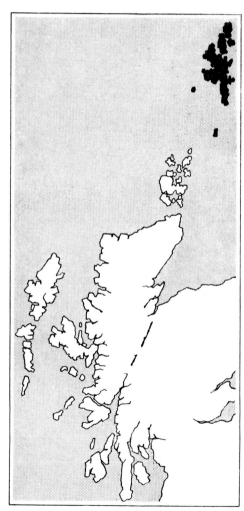

No one should visit the great Fair Isle Observatory without reading Ken Williamson's lovingly-written *Fair Isle and its Birds* in which you will learn that the recording of rarities and banding of passage migrants are small parts of a tremendous and continuing project. Enthusiasts have never allowed routine to become a chore. There is so much more to it than 'Ring and Fling'.

Fair Isle has added more species to the British list than has any other part of Britain. Ken Williamson casually mentions a few discoveries—in 1906 a thrush nightingale from south-east Asia, lanceolated warbler in 1925, citrine wagtail and a hen Baikal teal from Siberia in 1954, Hudsonian curlew in 1955, and western sandpiper and booted warbler in 1956.

The Observatory ringing list leaves me breathless. I have never seen, and hardly even heard of, some of these rarities. Yet finding, trapping, mist-netting, identifying and logging is only the beginning. Here they work on moults, aging and sexing, weighing and measuring, and on ectoparasites as well as assessing racial or specific characters of living birds. The work on ectoparasites particularly fascinates me. Between 1948-73 the Observatory staff and their willing helpers ringed 105,250 birds of which 1,085 have been recovered and are now on record.

But the Observatory has other tasks. We do not yet know whether the young sea eagles, which George Waterston and Johan Willgohs brought from Norway in autumn 1968 and released on the island, will finally succeed in nesting here or elsewhere in Scotland. The young ernes were slow to learn how to capture young fulmars; that deadly oil probably killed at least one of them. But we must persevere and learn from experience.

I could spend all my time with the arctic skuas about which Williamson and Peter Davis learnt so much. In 1954 there were thirty-four pairs, but in 1973 the colony had grown to about 106 pairs. What a lot they discovered about the breeding structure of these groups. Arctic skuas are three to five years old before they breed, but a three-year-old hen only lays a single egg. Young pairs often divorce, but older and more experienced pairs are more stable. The chance to pursue these earlier studies is surely too good to miss. Here arctic skuas are dominant and smaller bonxie groups on the wane.

But you may not wish to sit and watch. For many the attraction of Fair Isle lies in good companions and co-operative research. You might also see a merlin chasing a hoopoe, bee-eaters bee-eating from telephone wires, a Pallas's sandgrouse squatting in a ploughed field, or possibly a great bustard among a flock of sheep!

In maps and newspapers and on television, they often place the Shetlands in a little box as offshore islands near Aberdeen. What an insult! Here you will find some of the most exciting birds and haunts in Britain.

I was imprinted early. As a small boy I found three special bird books in the Linen Hall Library, Belfast. These I read and read again. In John Walpole-Bond's *Field Studies of*

The powerful bonxie or great skua in full flight. Bonxies often bully gannets and make them disgorge their fish, by tipping them over and sending them crashing into the sea.

Some Rarer British Birds I learnt about peregrines, hobbys and merlins and ravens, choughs and golden eagles. From this tremendous book I sensed the thrill of climbing high trees and going down great cliffs on ropes. Seton Gordon's *Hill Birds of Scotland*, which my grandmother later gave me as a birthday present, wove a different spell. I now first read about the Cairngorm Hills where cock snow buntings sometimes sang, and tame and fearless, colourful little dotterels ran over the rounded tops. A rather musty dog-eared volume, bound in maroon leather, also stirred me. How the Victorians did love pompous titles! *Birds of Shetland, with Observation of their Habits, Migrations and Occasional Appearance.* 'By the late Henry L. Saxby, M.D., of Balta Sound, Unst.' I read it quickly. What a banquet! These islands, hidden in grey mist and battered by Atlantic storms, held everything that an eager birdsnesting schoolboy could possibly desire. Step by step I followed the eccentric doctor as he searched distant islands or scaled cliffs to rob sea eagles of their eggs. Almost always the doctor was on the point of finding rare birds' nests, discovered nowhere else in Britain. Sea eagles and peregrines, whimbrels and red-necked phalaropes, bonxies and arctic skuas were not enough. Cunning and mysterious Shetlanders were always producing the unexpected or explaining why they hadn't. Sitting muffled in his gig or clopping along on his nag, the worthy doctor made 'contacts' on his rounds. They gave him 'freshly taken' snow buntings' eggs from Saxaford; but he somehow always just failed to see the nest. Turnstone, purple sandpiper and even knot all nested, or at least he 'obtained' their eggs, in the Shetland Isles. Great northern divers were also there, he thought. He carefully measured the eggs they gave him and then convinced himself, if almost no one else. With open palms and carrying small wooden boxes, tweedy dealers waited until surgery was over. Even now I can never quite decide whether old Saxby suffered from delusions or was a credulous, regionally-proud, and perhaps stingy old buffer, whom grasping Shetland birders delightedly exploited!

I have now fulfilled most of what I planned. I have watched all the birds about which Jock Bond wrote so lovingly. I have lived on the Cairngorm tops and among the flows of Sutherland, but Shetland is still a dream. For those who, like myself, are wader lovers, how exciting these islands are. I would gladly watch breeding whimbrels. How do whimbrels and curlews divide their habitats? What are the differences in their food and feeding ecology? Why do whimbrels nest in shorter herbage and in woolly fringemoss higher up the hills? Have these different habitats led to different patterns of eggshell disposal? Do whimbrels and curlews deal differently with predators and which breeds more successfully in Shetland and for what reasons?

How compelling also to compare the dotterel of the high hills with the red-necked phalaropes of these Shetland marshes. Both are birds with reversed courtships with the larger, brighter and dominant hens leaving the smaller cocks to brood the eggs and rear the chicks. In

Arctic skua at the nest. This dashing pirate has many large colonies in Shetland. Cambridge University researchers are studying the genetics and selection of the colour phases. This information will end up in computer language!

Shetland, do hen phalaropes hold territories, as Tinbergen found in Greenland or, as in Alaska, do they disperse by other means? Do hens ever brood and do they always quit their nesting marshes before the young can fly? What is the precise timing and pattern of the brooding rhythm? I could enjoy many summers with these lovely phalaropes. See that bright and gorgeous hen chasing the little cock. Now watch him dart across the marsh and drop down to the tiny nest and even smaller speckled pear-shaped eggs. Almost incomparably graceful these red-necks are as they pirouette on the little pools. I would also hope to see black-tailed godwits nesting on Unst and discover how, where, and with what they live.

And sometimes I dream dreams in which I watch a turnstone back to eggs or I see the flutter of wings as the first Shetland purple sandpiper rises at my feet!

But daydreams are futile. Watch red-throated divers and tape-record their strange music. Do some red-throats pair, but fail to breed as in parts of Sutherland? Do these pairs consist of immature birds or are some past or potential breeders?

I could gladly spend many years watching bonxies. What do we know about their population explosion? In 1887 only about sixty pairs bred on Foula but by 1969 these colonies had grown to 1,100-1,200 pairs. Many groups show the same rate of increase. Almost all the largest groups are sited close to vast congregations of kittiwakes and other sea-birds. Have sea-bird numbers greatly changed in the last 100 years or so? Is this why bonxies are spreading south so fast? Why not study the non-breeding groups and discover the proportion of potential breeders as against younger birds?

The graceful kittiwakes offer a lifetime of inquiry and research; or think of crowded twilight hours on the screes and banks of East Neap on Fetlar where the storm petrels are in hundreds.

There are many Shetland raptor problems. Why have golden eagles never taken the erne's place on the cliffs? Are fulmars really capable of destroying young eagles before they learn proper hunting techniques? Where do Shetland peregrines go in winter? Poisoned pigeons have possibly almost destroyed them. Are merlins also victims of DDT? Do their young winter on Shetland islands or do they go away to more contaminated habitats? Why has the kestrel gone, when, in old Saxby's time, it was quite a well-distributed breeding bird? Why do many hen harriers and short-eared owls breed in Orkney but none in Shetland? Is this all due to lack of voles in Shetland?

There is much to learn about passerines. How I should love to hear a cock snow bird singing on an Atlantic sea cliff or watch the hen flit to a nest in scree. All over Britain corn buntings are deserting former haunts. Why not critically examine occupied and recently-deserted habitats in Shetland and Orkney? How do rock and meadow pipits divide their habitats? Why are rock pipits restricted to coast and island and meadow pipits to open moors? How do they react to one another on their 'marches' and how do their diets differ? What large flocks of ravens there always were in Shetland. One June day on Unst, in the 1860's, 800 ravens assembled on some flenshed whales, and hundreds still gather on the Lerwick rubbish dumps. Even when hens are sitting eggs, parties of twenty or more are sometimes on the wander. Compare raven groups with those on Skye. Is their laying season related to the late Shetland lambing and do these hens lay their eggs fully three weeks later than those I knew in Devon and Cornwall? Shetland would be perfect for a comparative study. Why not catch and colourband those Lerwick flocks? Here hooded crows are bold and cheeky. Less persecuted than on the mainland grouse moors, they sometimes rob merlins' nests and pester snowy owls.

Now let us take a look at Shetland. In north Mainland snowy owls are sometimes seen on rocky ground on Ronas Hill where Bobby Tulloch hopes that they may nest. Great skuas already nest and dotterels might colonise a fine *rhacomitrium* heath on this hill. In April great northern divers often assemble on Ronas Voe below the hill and a few king eiders have occasionally shown up. On the east coast of north Mainland some arctic skuas and whimbrels are also scattered over the Girlsta heights.

On both sides of Eshaness Lighthouse thousands of fulmars nest on the cliffs and large colonies of great black-backs and herring gulls breed on offshore stacks. At Stenness immense groups of puffins haunt the lower cliffs and there are huge colonies of kittiwakes on the small island of Dore Holm. In 1968, at Ollaberry, fieldfares nested for the first time in Shetland.

The many lochs and tarns of west Mainland hold red-throated divers and a few scoters. On these desolate but attractive flows new discoveries are always likely. You should also visit the softer country and plantations of Weisdale Valley where fieldfares nested in 1969. These woods are great places for spotting spring and autumn migrants. Yellow-browed warblers and rustic buntings are among recent finds.

In south Mainland thousands of guillemots, razorbills and puffins breed on Sumburgh Head. North-west lie the fearsome cliffs of Fitful Head where peregrines used to have an eyrie, and where there are bonxie colonies on the slopes above. Loch Spiggie, a great haunt of wintering ducks and whooper swans, is also a Shetland phalarope loch. Do remember that southern Mainland is another wonderful place to find rare strays on their spring and autumn movements. Bobby Tulloch mentions red-breasted flycatchers and subalpine warblers.

The small island of Noss, east of Lerwick, is a magnificent sea-bird station. Several thousand pairs of gannets nest on the Noup where there are also teeming colonies of other sea-birds. Down below tysties nest in rocky hollows and under boulders. On grassy slopes above the cliffs about 200 pairs of bonxies and some arctic skuas have territories. These bonxies sometimes feed arctic skua chicks to their nestlings.

On the ground the great arctic snowy owl looks almost like a child's snowman. Probably because myxomatosis has decimated local rabbit colonies, these owls have to rear their chicks on oyster-catchers and other waders.

Mousa, a green island, has a wonderful Pictish broch in the drystone walls of which many storm petrels nest. In these old walls starlings, wrens, rock pipits, puffins, black guillemots, rock doves and fulmars also all have nesting niches. What a prize for any ecologist worth his salt!

The Island of Whalsay and the Out Skerries off the east coast are fine watching points for spring and autumn movements. On the Out Skerries in the last few years observers have logged 160 different kinds of birds, including short-toed lark, red-throated pipit, aquatic, icterine, barred, subalpine, yellow-browed and arctic warblers, bluethroats, ortolan, Lapland and little buntings, slate-coloured junco and scarlet rosefinch. In summer Whalsay is still better. Here on its hills, lochs and marshes exciting things are happening. Whimbrels have returned and are increasing; and golden plover, redshank and dunlin are nesting regularly in small numbers. Groups of red-throated divers have built up to about fifteen pairs; red-breasted mergansers, merlins and white wagtails breed sporadically; and in 1968 about sixty pairs of kittiwakes were nesting on Clett Head where they are still increasing. (J. H. Simpson.)

For long the dumpy hills and cliffs of Yell were an 'Eggers' Mecca'. I often think of the mysterious Anglican parson, dog-collar and all, arriving in 1910 with his climbing spikes to loot the last Shetland erne's eyrie on the Eigg near Whalefirth. And on the Sabbath too!

Here on Yell whimbrels regularly nested until the 1940's; and now more and more you again hear their silvery trill above the mosses. There are merlins on the hill, dunlins and golden plovers on the moors, and red-throated divers on inland tarns. Bonxies and arctic skuas nest freely and storm petrels breed among the fallen stones of a broch at Cuppaster. Yell may sometimes harbour even rarer breeding birds. On Basta Voe, on 26th August 1956, Venables watched a great northern loon swimming with a young bird beside it. Perhaps you will find the first Shetland nest here!

Heathery Fetlar is one of the best bird haunts in Britain. Good numbers of whimbrels and over twenty pairs of red-necked phalaropes nest on the island. Dunlins are in the mosses, oystercatchers and ringed plovers on inland hills, and snipe, curlew, lapwing and redshank on the lower ground. Great and arctic skuas from the hills of Lambhoga often harry the gannets passing to and from the cliffs of Hermaness. Here manx shearwaters and storm petrels breed in burrows on the grassy upper slopes and tysties in stone walls.

In 1967 that famous pair of snowy owls nested on the rocky hill of Stakkaberg. Bobby Tulloch's heart must have missed a beat when he saw those three round white eggs lying in the heather. But he caught his breath, held his tongue, and led his companions away. How many would have had his quickness of reaction!

What a lot you learn from the watchers' log-books! The cock hunted while the hen was brooding eggs, each of which took about thirty-three days to hatch. In every twenty-four hours the hen left the nest about half-a-dozen times to preen, void, and throw up pellets.

A teeming guillemot colony. Guillemots usually nest in packed communities where they often share eggs, chicks and mates. John Parslow's work at Clo Mor is mainly on guillemots and razorbills. "Adult survival has been high (especially for razorbill—of the order of 95 per cent survival in 1971-72 and again 1972-73), reproductive success is good (50 to 60 per cent chicks fledging from eggs laid), and return of pre-breeding birds ringed as chicks in 1971 and back in 1973 (none return at one year of age) is high."

The cock now sometimes took the chance to mate her; but he was also a good provider—twenty-five rabbits in twenty-three days. What lovely glimpses of the lives of these great white owls they give you! You can almost see the cock switch the prey from foot to beak and walk the few yards to offer it to the hen. Once the hen refused a small black rabbit, "turning her head resolutely away when he rubbed her face with it". In the end the huffy cock ate the rabbit himself, "whereupon the female poked underneath herself and produced a larger grey rabbit which she ate". The cock continued to hunt after the young had hatched, but the hen fed the owlets, at first gently passing tiny morsels to them. Once the cock tried to feed them in her absence, but she soon rushed back and, "snatching the rabbit from him", attended to their needs! In their first thirty-four days the cock supplied hen and chicks with fifty-nine rabbits, twenty-three oystercatchers, three curlews or whimbrels, one lapwing, and one arctic skua fledgling and fifteen other birds or mammals. The young owls made their first sustained flights after about forty-three or forty-four days in the nest; and the whole brood was strong on the wing by fifty days.

These fine snowy owls still breed on Fetlar. Bobby Tulloch tells me that in 1973 the cock had two wives, the younger of which he neglected. While she was hunting, hoodies broke an egg, and she deserted her nest. The old hen reared two owlets but only one survived.

The most northerly large island, Unst, is composed of nearly 30,000 acres of gneiss, gabbro and serpentine. Here are green and peaty hills, huge sea cliffs, and many lochs and sheltered voes. In our northern isles only Fetlar and Mainland Orkney are its peers. In the early 1950's over thirty pairs of whimbrels nested; and there are still more there today. On the western gneiss, with its peat and heather, are skylarks and meadow pipits, with merlins, arctic skuas and bonxies as their predators. On voes and coast and on inland lochs the striking black-and-white drake eider courts and croons. See him raise his head and neck and jerk up his beak to excite the duck!

In the north are fine cliffs, particularly around Hermaness, which is now a Nature Reserve. One mile offshore is lonely Muckle Flugga with its famous gannetry of several thousand pairs. Now breeding in hundreds on the Head of Hermaness, bonxies harry the gannets and rob kittiwakes' eggs and chicks. What vicious brutes these great skuas are! They sometimes feed arctic skua nestlings to their chicks. I have heard that arctics sometimes do the same!

But Unst offers other treasures and exciting prospects. In 1949 black-tailed godwits nested on a marsh and now breed quite regularly. Good naturalists have seen pairs of snow buntings on the Hill of Saxaford in summer, but we still await the first authentic nest. One day someone will find turnstones nesting on the rocky east coast and perhaps purple sandpipers on some stony hill. Old Dr Saxby certainly knew what he was about when he courted the laird's daughter and put up his plate at Balta Sound in Unst.

Opposite: The sea-cliffs of Fair Isle where young sea-eagles were re-introduced from Norway in 1968, but they failed to settle.

Below left: Puffin with fish in its beak of many colours. Puffins nest in immense colonies where they brood their single sparsely-marked eggs in burrows for about forty-two days. In one Shetland haunt many puffins are known to lay handsome well-coloured eggs.

Below centre: You will enjoy looking at these great groups of gannets and guillemots nesting on immense sea cliffs.

Below right: 'Watch the striking black and white drake eider court and croon. See him raise head and neck and jerk up his beak to excite the duck.'

Opposite: 'Over thirty years ago I fell in love with the greenshank and lived happily ever after.' To me, there is no field sport quite like tracking down its nest.

Bottom left: Whimbrel about to brood. One of our rarest breeding waders, but there are now about 150 pairs in their headquarters on the Shetland islands. In recent years it has also nested in Orkney, Sutherland and Easter Ross, and on Lewis, St Kilda and Fair Isle.

Below right: The nesting of a pair of snowy owls on Fetlar in 1967 was a major sensation. Snowy owls are now prospecting other breeding haunts in the Highlands and Islands. Here is the hen's distraction display.

92

The clutch of three erythristic (red) herring gulls eggs, with a normal egg for comparison (about one-half natural size). These were the first erythristic herring gull's eggs recorded from Scotland; the few others all came from Scandinavia.

Opposite page: left: The huge cliffs of Clo Mor, east of Cape Wrath lighthouse. While you watch the packed sea-bird colonies here you will also see streams of gannets passing to and from their fishing grounds.

Opposite page: right: Fulmar brooding. For about eight weeks cock and hen in turn brood the single egg usually for spells of two-and-a-half to five days.

Below left: Wood sandpiper among cotton sedge on a Sutherland flow. In these decades of cooling climate these lovely boreal waders have started to nest in the Scottish Highlands.

Below right: Black-throated diver on eggs in a shallow scrape. This is one of the most dramatic and colourful birds found on Highland lochs.

Left: A Caithness dubhlochan haunt of dunlins.

Centre: The high Torridonian sandstone cliffs of Handa where fulmars, great black-backed and herring gulls, kittiwakes, and auks nest in great numbers. On this R.S.P.B. Reserve red-throated divers, bonxies, and sometimes arctic skuas, and ravens nest.

Right: A characteristic Sutherland flow with the formidable peaks of Ben Loyal in the background. There are golden eagles and ravens on Ben Loyal and greenshanks and divers on many flows.

Caithness and Sutherland

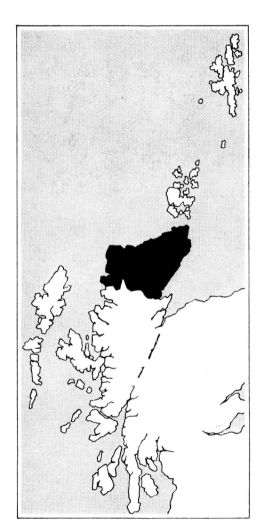

Caithness is a county of contrasts. In the north-east are rich farmlands and many lochs, with familiar birds like swifts, swallows and martins, thrushes, blackbirds, lapwings and black-headed gulls. Farther west, wild bleak flows and hills stretch right across Caithness to Strath More in Sutherland and beyond. In this frightening and infinitely lonely grey-brown wilderness black-throated and red-throated divers nest among lochs and tarns. A few greenshanks also nest, but in early June 1969, Derek Ratcliffe walked fifteen miles over the great flows of Blar nan Faoileag to the Dubh Lochs of Shielton without hearing or seeing one. Golden plovers are on drier moors, groups of dunlins haunt small water holes and the lochans; and a few scoters also nest in these Caithness bogs.

In 1969 Thurso bird-watchers discovered a new colony of arctic skuas in Caithness where a few scattered pairs and small nesting groups were already known. In 1952, I. D. Pennie described the Watten colony as nesting "in a trackless and seemingly endless and bottomless morass thickly studded with dubhlochans". How beautifully these skuas distract you with their broken-wing tricks; and how they fly, darting, flashing and turning with complete mastery of the air.

Bonxies are recent settlers at Dunnet Head where a few pairs nest near arctic skua groups. These powerful birds may also establish themselves on moors and slopes behind other sea cliffs.

From 1946 onwards black-tailed godwits have sometimes nested on coastal moors in north Caithness. Here you always hope to find them. Watch also for whimbrels on round hills and grassy flows. In 1969 a pair probably bred here. In this huge country of mysterious charm do keep looking for wood sandpipers, Temminck's stints, and other sub-arctic waders. Go to the many bird lochs. Slavonian grebes nest on one of them. On 13th June 1969 a dozen were in residence. Gadwalls and pochards are also sometimes found here. These lochs attract unusual visitors. On 12th July 1967 a white-winged black tern mobbed observers and in another year a friend saw a red-necked phalarope in June. In north Caithness there are also up to sixty pairs of greylag geese, the largest groups in mainland Britain.

On burn and river are beautiful mergansers and goosanders and dippers bob on stones and rocks. Sandpipers flicker beside rivers and open water. Pied wagtails grace many streams, but grey wagtails are scarcer. All these lovely birds belong to warm midgy evenings against a background chorus of dunlins and golden plovers.

A pair of golden eagles and ravens haunt inland crags. Sparrowhawks and long-eared owls are in conifer plantations and broad-leaved woods in Berriedale and Langwell. In 1968 D. M. Stark recorded two pairs of tree-nesting ravens; one pair nested in an isolated fir plantation, the second in a sycamore wood.

In Caithness woodlands blue and great tits are commonest; coal tits breed in smaller numbers; and long-tailed tits are occasional winter visitors. Wood pigeons dominate the conifers and collared doves are colonising. Wood warblers have nested; whitethroats and willow warblers fluctuate; and a few sedge warblers chatter in swamps. Twites still nest in fair numbers round old and new croftlands. On 12th May 1968 observers saw a pied fly-catcher and in June 1969 a grasshopper warbler sang near Reay. Will both these birds soon nest in Caithness?

You must visit the sea cliffs, which are the greatest pride of Caithness. Here peregrines are doing better—three broods fledged in 1969. Along these cliffs are good colonies of razorbills, guillemots, kittiwakes and fulmars. You will find the Heads of Dunnet, Duncansby, Holbourn and Noss are grand sea-bird watching-points. Near Brough fulmars ousted herring gulls from their traditional cliffs. The dispossessed gulls then nested on tilled fields behind. Most exciting is the colony of 10,000 pairs of kittiwakes at Boch-ailean, one and a half miles south-west of Berriedale. The Caithness coast also holds the largest Scottish breeding colony of cormorants. Near the Ord of Caithness 400-500 pairs nest on both sides of the Caithness-Sutherland march in separated groups, usually of not less than twenty pairs; but in 1967 there were two concentrations, each with over seventy nests. About two miles north some twenty pairs nest on a 500-foot cliff, and on the stacks of Mid Clyth, north of Lybster, is another colony of fifty pairs.

A few herons still nest on Caithness cliffs "but the numbers nesting are sadly depleted although the actual numbers of birds seen has not fallen. They may be using new sites but we have not yet located them". (D. M. Stark.) Do try to find these heronries. It is always fun to watch herons nesting on big sea cliffs. They seem so small, strange, and out of place. In rocky and sandy bays are many oystercatchers and some ringed plovers. In 1968 little terns bred at the mouth of Webster Burn. Look for sandwich terns. There is almost certainly an undiscovered colony somewhere along this coast.

In autumn and winter eider and long-tailed duck are quite plentiful on the north coast. Goldeneye and merganser also gather. Sandside Bay sometimes holds 200 wigeon and a few teal and mallard. Inland lochs around Wick and Dunnet have also attracted 1,000 mallard, wigeon, and quite large numbers of teal and diving ducks. Pochard, goldeneye, tufted duck, a few pintail and small herds of mute and whooper swans have also been recorded. But in winter moorland lochs in south and west Caithness hold few wildfowl.

Sutherland is probably the wildest and most romantic county in Scotland. To me, there is nothing to compare with these vast grey-brown flows. In Central Sutherland big hills squat like huge cups in deep saucers and in the south-west Suilven and Canisp stand up like sore thumbs. On flows below the hills are the lochs and tarns which set the hunters tramping ever since men went north for birds. These old trophy-hunters, hardy and resourceful men, came in carriages and traps, bringing indiarubber boats to explore the lochs. They also carried guns and had drills and blowpipes in their satchels. In 1902 Norman Gilroy, the great nester, started hunting greenshanks on flows near Altnaharra. When I drive from Lairg to Tongue I can almost see the stocky figure with the egg-shaped head and bright blue eyes, and field glasses always at the ready. His pioneer paper on the greenshank pointed the way that I have followed.

In 1932 I was in Strath Helmsdale. I can still feel my sense of acute loneliness and of infinite smallness as I fought and lost my first battle with the greenshank in immense tarn-studded flows below the Griams. In this huge country, part of the Great Bog of Sutherland, I once watched a golden eagle chase a raven for several miles. The raven croaked and flapped, but the eagle was gaining when I saw the two birds disappear over a hill.

In early morning and late evening, greenshanks start nestward flights from loch or river. Here golden plovers pipe in mournful chorus and the cocks sing and challenge high above grassland moors. A few scoters nest in the wetter mosses and teal are not uncommon. You might even watch the songflight of wood sandpipers or hear the trill of a Temminck's stint. In 1962 I watched a Temminck's stint but failed to find the nest. Whimbrels have already nested.

Black-throated divers prefer larger lochs and red-throats the peaty tarns. A few greylag geese still nest; in June 1970 we saw three pairs with broods swimming beside a busy road. The same day two full-grown young oystercatchers swam across a tranquil loch. Common gulls nest on flows and river-shingle and a few black-heads haunt the dubhlochans and have large colonies on some wetlands.

Men are now changing the face of the Great Bog. New forests grow on many drier edges and already block out the great open spaces. Some greenshank ground is lost and gone, but hen harriers court and somersault and short-eared owls drop down to broods in young plantations.

The flat and cliffless coast of south-east Sutherland greatly differs from the north and west.

On dune and shingle soft-winged ringed plovers turn and swerve in courtship flights and on the ground cocks 'mark time' behind their hens. Here you also watch the complex piping displays of seapies. Common terns have colonies, but the erratic sandwich tern comes and goes. There are wildfowl and wader refuges on the southern coast of Sutherland. Rare strays sometimes arrive here. On 18th April 1970, Donnie Macdonald and Valerie Thom watched a stilt sandpiper on Dornoch saltmarsh, a first for Scotland and the first spring record for the British Isles. A wader of the North American arctic tundra, the stilt sandpiper normally winters in South America. At Dornoch it was a stranger in a strange land. In spring many long-tailed duck assemble off Dornoch and in late summer and autumn the mergansers

100

also gather. At Embo there are sometimes flocks of over 1,000 common and velvet scoters. Many long-tailed duck concentrate in Golspie Bay and mergansers winter off the flat Brora coast. Eiders group at the entrance to Loch Fleet where the Mound Alderwoods Nature Reserve is another refuge. You should work these fine alder swamps in summer; no one really knows what they contain. Below the Mound shelducks nest in scree and on bracken-covered slopes. In 1973 a red-necked grebe was here in August and a king eider in November.

Inland south Sutherland is attractive. In the woods you watch the turkey cock displays of capercaillies and hear blackcocks at lek. Work these woods and enjoy the cock siskins joy-flying above the pines. In 1970 I proved that Scottish parrot crossbills were nesting in these woods. Perhaps you will also find the first crested tit's nest in Sutherland. These attractive little birds have long nested just across the county march.

Goldcrests, coal tits, creepers and greenfinches are common in the pines; lesser redpolls, great and blue tits are in the oaks and birches, and lovely chaffinches dominate all these woods. Ring doves coo and 'clap'; one cock sang and fed on the ground almost beside me as I quietly waited for a building siskin to return. In older woods pied woodpeckers drum; cock redstarts entice hens to nesting stumps in sunny places; and tree pipits rise, sing and parachute from scattered trees. Yellowhammers jingle in the brush and reed buntings are in squashy places. In a few young plantations grasshopper warblers sing but no one has yet found nest or brood here. Wood warblers trill in at least one fine old oakwood. How lovely to find them here and how they remind me of summer days spent in Sussex and Surrey woods long ago! Always look and listen for bramblings in the birches. In June 1968 two cocks were singing not far from where that first pair had nested in 1920. In old oaks, wet birches and alders, also look out for pied flycatchers and listen for willow tits in really soggy woods. Blackcaps and garden warblers occasionally sing in shrubberies; chiffchaffs are extremely rare, but whitethroats are often common round the edges. These woods also have larger birds. Hoodies and carrion crows defy the gamekeepers and buzzards and sparrowhawks still maintain. One young pine plantation holds a small heronry. In 1969 keepers were shooting these handsome birds and destroying their young.

My friend, Donnie Macdonald, studied the corn buntings around Dornoch for many years. Now, in 1973, he could not locate a single pair. Scottish ornithologists should seek the causes of this decline, for these dull-brown and heavy-looking buntings are really among our most exciting birds. Look out for the cock standing on a tall weed, gatepost or telegraph wire and listen to his incessant song sounding like a bunch of heavy keys shaken together. Sit down or stand on a bank and never take your eyes off him. Suddenly you hear a sharp *chit* and see that he is off and flying fast. See, he is chasing the hen who has left her eggs unseen and is off to feed. Stay put! Give your corn buntings a few minutes and they should come flying back, quite low above the ground, the cock still flying in fast pursuit. He now swings up

on to his singing post and the hen rises in a curve and lands on a tall weed in open field. For a minute or two she flicks her tail, then she flies down and disappears. Mark her. Now gently flick around with your stick. Wings flutter just ahead. There in the loosely-built nest, almost at your feet, are four or five pale-grounded eggs marked with Chinese hieroglyphics. Go back and watch. You have only started. This is what bird-watching is all about. Some cocks are polygamous, one in north Cornwall had a harem of seven hens. In Sutherland a few cocks also had two wives, but few of them helped to feed the chicks.

The south-east Sutherland hinterland is rewarding. Fulmars float round the Mound and Carrol Rock and crags in Strath Fleet. Golden eagles have eyries in several glens. D. Bremner, our best and keenest peregrine watcher, has seen the dramatic mating, with the tiercel landing on the falcon's back and then swooping down the cliff.

On the way to deer-grass country you pass colonies of black-headed gulls; and on one small inland loch great black-backed gulls have nested on one islet and black-throated divers on another. Here common terns have also sometimes nested far from the sea. On these flat or undulating brown and yellow heaths, golden plovers and red grouse and meadow pipits and skylarks nest at higher density than in the west Sutherland gneiss country. How marvellously these skylarks mock the greenshanks. I have often been deceived! Greenshanks are fewer than in the west and curlews are scarce or missing from these deer-grass flats where I am always expecting whimbrels to nest.

This is real osprey country. In the late 1960's I watched them fishing and soaring over the hills and woods where they later nested.

Some good marshes still exist in Sutherland. I have watched whooper swans in spring, but I leave you to find the first nest. In 1848 Charles St John heard bitterns booming on the Shinness marshes. In these years, I suppose, bitterns and marsh harriers are not impossible. From 1966 to 1970 spotted crakes called in a deep and filthy north-west Sutherland mire. Here the cock 'whiplashed' every year but the eager searchers never found the nest or chicks. Some day a daring nester will find how to defeat the bog. I should love to see his face when he looks down at that first Sutherland spotted crake's nest and eggs!

In 1886 B. N. Peach and Lionel Hinxman, the famous geologists, located the first recorded Scottish snow bunting's nest on the quartzite screes of Ben More Assynt in south-west Sutherland. There also, two years later, John Young found the first and only Sutherland nest with eggs. The nest was hidden on a scree slope "so loose that the greatest caution was necessary to avoid stones falling on one—large stones rolling down at the slightest touch".

Watch for dotterels on all broad ridges. In 1967 a Sheffield girl, on a Kyle and Glen Highland Safari, found the only dotterel's nest ever recorded in Sutherland. Dotterels have been seen in summer on at least three other hills; in 1973 a pair courted on one great ben.

For those who prefer the lower ground, search the huge flows on both sides of Loch Shin. Hill lochs near Lairg offer prospects. Booth saw red-necked phalaropes on one of them; and I have a record of a hen seen not long ago. Explore also the coast, islands and vast hinterland between Melvich and Durness, where, on a June day in 1973, Derick Scott watched a whimbrel run back to eggs.

It is an unusual and exciting journey by ferry and minibus and on foot to the Parphe and hills around Cape Wrath. Greenshanks nest on the flows, ptarmigan on the tops, and bonxies are colonising. A few miles east of Cape Wrath are the tremendous sea-bird cliffs of Clo Mor. Large colonies of puffins nest on grassy slopes and thousands of guillemots brood on broad ledges. Under rocks and crevices lower down the cliff are many razorbills and on narrow ledges, almost inaccessible to all but the boldest cragsman, are clusters of kittiwakes. Fulmars float round the cliffs and nest on narrow ledges. Herring gulls are here in hundreds and great black-backs have large colonies on stacks. Many shags nest along the shore. On these fine mainland sea-cliffs John Parslow has placed coloured bands on guillemots and razorbills. He seeks deeper knowledge of their populations and ecology. For sheer size, clamour and excitement Clo Mor is my favourite Scottish mainland sea-bird cliff.

On the Island of Handa the R.S.P.B. has a Reserve with simple bothies and a minimum of direction. On a 'picture postcard' day in August 1968, I took the children there. Herring gulls were their usual yelling selves; arctic terns fished; and tysties swam lazily beside the boat. On ledges of the Torridonian sandstone cliffs fulmars had chicks. We watched their greeting ritual and listened to them cackling. Huge groups of razorbills, guillemots and kittiwakes were on the Great Stack. Kittiwakes were lower down on narrow ledges. Great black-backed and herring gulls were everywhere. Puffins flew on quick wings or stood with fish in parrot beaks. As the children fired questions at me how I wished that I knew more about social birds! In these gull 'cities' each pair holds a territory of a few square feet, without which it cannot breed. Yet all these teeming thousands have independent lives and special relationships with near neighbours. Ravens croaked and tumbled overhead, gulls challenged hunting bonxies, and red-throated divers wailed on a little tarn. In the evening Ian Munro of Dollar showed us the bonxies. We tape-recorded their *tuk-tuk* mobbing cries and saw a young one make its first weak flight. In the moss a sharp-winged arctic skua with chicks scolded us. We had all loved Handa.

Sutherland sea-bird colonies have riches. In May 1969 Neville Cuss was on an island. "Arriving at the last colony of herring gulls, I was astonished to see three red eggs in the

Look at the raindrops on this lapwing's back. In early spring lapwings often take up their territories by moonlight. Watch the gorgeous cock frantically rocking to entice a hen. And what exciting love lives they have!

nearest nest. I looked and looked and could hardly believe my eyes! A few minutes later the herring gulls came back and one settled down on those fantastic eggs!"

Dr Hugh Blair, our greatest expert on erythrism in gulls' eggs, writes: "Herring gulls' eggs show a wide range of variation. Certainly the most attractive are the examples of erythrism with their white, buff or pinkish shells, blotched and spotted in shades of red and violet. The more boldly-marked call to mind the eggs of the birds of prey; and the first to reach Britain were actually offered for sale as eagle's eggs! Until Mr Cuss's discovery such striking varieties have been found only in Scandinavia and all but a few are from the gulleries of Arctic Norway. As Olson has shown by tracing and ringing birds, a herring gull will occasionally join a flock from a colony far from that at which it broke the shell, then follow its new companions when they return to their breeding haunts, and there find a mate. Surely then we may consider the possibility of the Sutherland erythristic eggs being laid by a hen hatched well to the north on some Norwegian cliff or island. Abroad, erythrism has been recorded with the greater black-backed, common, and Iceland gulls. The only other gull known to have laid erythristic eggs in Britain is the black-headed gull. Three fine examples from a Sutherland gullery are well figured in Harvie-Brown and Buckley's *Vertebrate Fauna of Sutherland, Caithness and West Cromarty* (p. 230)."

Sutherland has done us proud!

Over thirty years ago I fell in love with the greenshank and have lived happily ever after. To me, this is the most wonderful bird that flies. Even now I never go out to watch it without the same urgency and excitement that I first felt in Strath Helmsdale. What a dramatic song flight the cock greenshank has! High in air, sometimes in the clouds, a small dark gnat-like thing soars and switchbacks, and all the time he sings his wild ecstatic song. This display has special uses. Just before the hen lays her first egg the cock particularly proclaims himself to warn off rivals from his territory.

But you should see the greenshanks make love. Watch that cock court his hen on the stony river bank. See him raise silver-lined wings and slowly goosestep towards her. Calling in short growling peals he beats his wings faster and faster as he advances. Then he stands just behind her until his flapping wings at last lift and drop him on her back, or watch him bow to her with upraised tail spread like a fan and his rump patch dazzling white and see him hold a wing over her just before he takes her.

Come late April and early May I am always with my greenshanks. There is no field sport quite like tracking down their nests and discovering how each pair behaves. I sometimes watch them choose and line their nests and even lay their eggs. For a few minutes the flow then rings with wild whistles and strange sobbing cries. "But when they are sitting how very different it all is. The brooding bird, perfectly camouflaged, lies somewhere on eggs—a

106

tiny pinpoint in a wilderness of stony desolation. Its mate, feeding or sleeping by the water's
edge, seldom visits her. Perhaps twice, or even once only, in the whole day, it flies up into
the hills to relieve the other at a nest which may be two or more miles away". On its eggs the
brooding greenshank sits like wax, looking exactly like one of the grey stones beside it.
In this huge cold wilderness of countless stones and rocks, searching is almost useless. You
must sit and wait until you hear faint chipping cries, barely heard against the wind. But
how elusive and difficult these are to place! You will spend many cold nights or early
mornings before you find the long-billed grey bird crouching and panting on its eggs or
watch it jump from its nest almost beside your feet.

In May and June these last eleven years we have all 'migrated' to a small fishing hut miles
from any road. Here we have some special birds in our little group of greenshanks. *Beauty*
allowed me to fondle her speckled throat as she sat on eggs. The *Tiger* and *Tigress* almost
beat me. I had never met such a cunning pair. Time after time I thought that I had won,
but all that I heard were almost mocking cries. Sometimes I sat down and almost wept.
Then, one night, as I crouched behind a rock, I saw the *Tiger* running up the hill, but I lost
him in the shadows. Still I now knew where to search. Next morning I walked the gneiss and
at last found the *Tigress* proudly sitting on nest and well-chipped eggs in a crack between
two lumps of rock.

On 28th May 1969 we found our 200th greenshank's nest. For three long days we had vainly
struggled. On the third night young Patrick and I saw the hen flash down the corrie,
clearly off a nest. With a few wild calls she flipped down to the river far below, but the waiting
cock had spotted us. Flying in circles and sometimes singing in the gathering mist, he
chipped and *chipped*, but it was almost dark before he started his nestward run, and we lost
him among the stones. Next day for hours we combed the quartzite screes without success.
Then, about a furlong from where the cock had started to run, the hen rose with a piercing
cry just below my boot!

I have taped the cries of exchanging greenshanks and have learnt that parents flying above
the nest use special squeaks to warn chicks still in eggs. Cocks which lose their hens sometimes find new mates within a fortnight. We are learning more about dispersion and about
these extra hens. We are also studying what these greenshanks eat. This is not nearly as
easy as it sounds. Richard is our expert at finding pellets!

In our wild and lovely valley days pass far too quickly. About half a mile behind the hut a
pair of golden eagles have eyries on a big cliff. We watch the eagles hunting and discover how
they feed their young. Dippers nest, mergansers court, and sandpipers mate almost beside us.
On warm evenings we listen to ring ouzels singing and hear them chattering near their nests.
On the flows are little groups of dunlin and golden plover and in the high gneiss red-throated

divers groan and roll-growl on tiny lochs. In stony corries ptarmigan belch and snow buntings have been seen in summer. Ospreys have fished the river. In 1966 I watched a golden eagle leave its nesting cliff to chase a fishing osprey. The osprey easily avoided the eagle's rush and soon soared over the cliffs and far away, but before it went I again heard those nostalgic cries which the Old Naturalists used to hear in Sutherland.

I still had one ambition—a wood sandpiper's nest with eggs! In 1969 Bruin and I waited in a wet flow in a different forest. In the evening we heard a wood sandpiper sing and saw him high in air. On tremulous wings he rose and dipped, sometimes almost overhead, at others far away. But we never lost him. We watched and watched until the tears streamed down our cheeks. Suddenly he dived into a distant flow where he stood on a grassy mound. For nearly twenty minutes we endured the evening midges but they beat us in the end. As I lit a match our bird vanished. We searched and searched until it was too dark to see. Next day we had better luck. In the evening the wood sandpiper flew in and vanished below a ridge. A few minutes later the pair began to sing and flew towards a loch. Soon one had returned along the ridge and dropped into broken ground. Hearts in mouths we marked the spot and started out to search. Suddenly, just between us, the wood sandpiper flicked off its nest. Then it *chipped* and sang and hovered only a few feet above our heads. With thumping heart and shaking knees I had to walk away. The Great Bog of Sutherland had been so kind to me!

Index

108

110